ROUTLEDGE LIBRARY EDITIONS: WOMEN IN SOCIETY

Volume 15

WOMEN SERVANTS OF THE STATE 1870–1938

WOMEN SERVANTS OF THE STATE 1870–1938

A History of Women in the Civil Service

HILDA MARTINDALE

LONDON AND NEW YORK

First published in 1938 by George Allen & Unwin Ltd

This edition first published in 2025
by Routledge
4 Park Square, Milton Park, Abingdon, Oxon OX14 4RN

and by Routledge
605 Third Avenue, New York, NY 10158

Routledge is an imprint of the Taylor & Francis Group, an informa business

© 1938 Hilda Martindale

All rights reserved. No part of this book may be reprinted or reproduced or utilised in any form or by any electronic, mechanical, or other means, now known or hereafter invented, including photocopying and recording, or in any information storage or retrieval system, without permission in writing from the publishers.

Trademark notice: Product or corporate names may be trademarks or registered trademarks, and are used only for identification and explanation without intent to infringe.

British Library Cataloguing in Publication Data
A catalogue record for this book is available from the British Library

ISBN: 978-1-032-87216-2 (Set)
ISBN: 978-1-032-86313-9 (Volume 15) (hbk)
ISBN: 978-1-032-86320-7 (Volume 15) (pbk)
ISBN: 978-1-003-52238-6 (Volume 15) (ebk)

DOI: 10.4324/9781003522386

Publisher's Note
The publisher has gone to great lengths to ensure the quality of this reprint but points out that some imperfections in the original copies may be apparent.

Disclaimer
The publisher has made every effort to trace copyright holders and would welcome correspondence from those they have been unable to trace.

WOMEN SERVANTS OF THE STATE 1870–1938

A History of Women in the Civil Service

by

HILDA MARTINDALE

C.B.E.

formerly of the Home Office and H.M. Treasury

Foreword by
THE RIGHT HON. THE
EARL BALDWIN OF BEWDLEY
K.G.

London
GEORGE ALLEN & UNWIN LTD
Museum Street

FIRST PUBLISHED IN 1938

All rights reserved
PRINTED IN GREAT BRITAIN BY
UNWIN BROTHERS LTD., WOKING

TO THOSE MEN WHO HAVE ENCOURAGED WOMEN
IN RENDERING SERVICE TO THE STATE
THIS BOOK IS DEDICATED

FOREWORD

IT is not so very long ago that all responsible and important work in the Civil Service was reserved for men, but of recent years there has been a marked tendency—perhaps even to a greater extent in the Civil Service than in most walks of life—for women to have a growing share, and judging by their performance there is no reason to question the rightness of this tendency or the likelihood of its further development.

The functions of government have widened and the activities of the Civil Service to-day touch the lives of the people at a thousand points. In connection with health and the care of women and children there are endless opportunities for the special aptitudes and gifts that belong to women and it surely must be that the country will in the future benefit more and more from the joint contribution to its service which can be made by the harmonious co-operation of men and women.

BALDWIN OF BEWDLEY

69, EATON SQUARE, S.W.
July 14, 1938

PREFACE

MANY of the men and women who have helped to make the history recorded in this book are still in the service or have retired within a comparatively short time, so it has seemed more fitting not to mention them individually. Also work in the Civil Service is largely team work, and to pick out certain persons may well become invidious. If they happen to read this volume they will easily recognize their particular contribution.

For some years it has seemed to me that a short history of the work that women have done for the State during the last seventy years might be of interest—a history which, as far as I know, has not been written. The number of colleagues—men and women—and friends who have helped in one way or another in the preparation of this book are too many to be mentioned by name. They all know that they have indeed my gratitude.

I must, however, single out those of my colleagues who have read particular chapters or the volume as a whole. I desire to mention Miss E. Sanday, O.B.E., Miss L. W. Wamsley, O.B.E., Miss C. L. Callis, Sir Hubert Llewellyn Smith, G.C.B., Miss C. Collet, and Miss M. Ritson, C.B.E., who have read and commented on individual chapters; and to thank especially the following who have given time and thought to reading the book as a whole—Sir Malcolm Delevingne, K.C.B., K.C.V.O., Miss E. G. Woodgate, O.B.E., Sir Gerald Bellhouse, C.B.E., and Miss H. C. Escreet.

I am indebted to Miss M. E. Bulkley for her help with the manuscript and careful attention to the proofs.

July, 1938   HILDA MARTINDALE

ACKNOWLEDGMENTS

IN writing a history of Women in the Civil Service, it has of course been necessary to draw largely on official publications. A list of these is given in the Bibliography, and I am indebted to the Controller of H.M. Stationery Office for giving permission to reproduce extracts from them.

The Board of Education Inspectors' Association have kindly allowed me to make use of their publication on the Development of the Inspectorate of the Board of Education, by H. E. Boothroyd, and the General Post Office have given similar permission in regard to the April 1913 number of *St. Martin's-le-Grand*.

I desire also to thank the publishers of the following works for permission to quote from them:—

Women as Civil Servants (The Nineteenth Century and After, Ltd., September 1881);

Women in the Factory, by Dame Adelaide Anderson, D.B.E. (Mr. John Murray);

Post Office, by Sir Evelyn Murray, K.C.B. (Messrs. Putnam & Company, Ltd.);

Women of the War, by Barbara McLaren (Messrs. Hodder & Stoughton, Ltd.);

Women Workers in Seven Professions, edited by Professor Edith Morley (Messrs. George Routledge & Sons, Ltd.);

and also Lady Spielman for similar permission in regard to her late husband's book, *The Romance of Child Reclamation*.

H. M.

CONTENTS

CHAPTER	PAGE
FOREWORD	9
PREFACE	11
ACKNOWLEDGMENTS	12
I. EARLY DAYS	15

Post Office—Local Government Board—Board of Education—Board of Trade—Home Office—National Health Insurance Commission—Shorthand and Typing Grades—Royal Commission on the Civil Service, 1912-1915

II. THE YEARS OF THE WAR	75
III. POST-WAR SETTLEMENT AND REORGANIZATION	87
IV. WOMEN IN THE TREASURY CLASSES	103

Administrative Class—Executive Class—Clerical Class—Writing Assistants and Shorthand-typists—Special Posts for Women

V. WOMEN IN THE DEPARTMENTS ... 114

Post Office—Ministry of Health—Board of Education—Ministry of Labour—Unemployment Assistance Board—Home Office—Ministry of Agriculture—Board of Inland Revenue and Estate Duty Office—Other Departments

VI. THE MARRIAGE BAR	146
VII. PAY AND SUPERANNUATION	158
VIII. THREE OUTSTANDING PERSONALITIES	176

Miss M. C. Smith—Miss M. H. Mason—Dame Adelaide Anderson, D.B.E.

IX. FUTURE OPPORTUNITIES OF SERVICE ... 187

Diplomatic and Consular Services—Colonial and Dominions Offices

IMPORTANT DATES	205
BIBLIOGRAPHY	209
INDEX	213

CHAPTER I

EARLY DAYS

WHAT is a civil servant? No authoritative answer has ever been given to this question, but the following may be taken as a working definition: "Civil servants are those servants of the Crown, other than holders of political or judicial offices, who are employed in a civil capacity and whose remuneration is paid wholly and directly out of moneys voted by Parliament." But a mere working definition is not enough. The Civil Service, as we know it, as *The Times* pointed out in a leading article, dates only from 1855. "At that date the British people—with the gravest misgivings, which their Queen shared—made up its mind to have its laws administered by professionals"; but these professionals were to be humane, to have a sense of the individual case behind the general law, to merge themselves among the people. This they have done, and so to-day "the English people have called into existence the acknowledged pattern of all Civil Services," constituted not of a separate official caste with rights and privileges not shared by the governed, but made up of ordinary men and women—chosen servants of the State.

THE POST OFFICE

On February 5th, 1870, the telegraph system in this country passed to the Controller of the Post Office, and by this act women for the first time became civil servants.

The telegraph services had grown up round the railway

system and were worked independently by a number of separate companies. Some of these, in particular the Electric and International Telegraph Company, employed women operators. According to a statement quoted in the *Englishwoman's Review* in 1873, it was owing to a suggestion made twenty years earlier to General Wylde by the Queen, who, "together with most of her daughters, it has long been understood . . . is in full sympathy with us in the struggle to open up sources of remunerative labour for women," that the employment of girls in telegraph offices was first entertained. "The offices of the Electric and International Telegraph Company, it would appear, were induced to evince their loyalty rather than their faith in women by engaging girls to the number of six." This was slowly followed up, and in 1870 there were 201 female workers at the central station.

The Telegraph Act of 1869 granted the Postmaster-General a monopoly of inland telegraph business, while he, on his part, became obliged, if so required, to purchase any existing telegraph companies. He was thus obliged to purchase the services of the women operators. Fortunately many of these operators had been carefully chosen, owing to the formation in 1859 of the Society for Promoting the Training of Women, under the presidentship of Lord Shaftesbury. To this society Queen Victoria was an early subscriber, thus showing her continued interest in the subject. One of its objects was "to substitute for competition in starvation a competition in skill," and one of the new employments to which applicants were introduced was the telegraph service. Thus, when the Post Office became the pioneer department in the employment of women in the

EARLY DAYS

Government service, they took over a number of women who had ventured into a new field of work and had left behind the overcrowded occupations of teaching and domestic work, which alone had been open to them.

The reorganization of the telegraph system was in astute hands. Mr. Scudamore, a Post Office official of eminence, realized at once that in the services of women there was an asset which might prove extremely useful in the task he had in front of him. The telegraph companies had employed women as operators, but he conceived the idea of entrusting clerical work also to them. In 1871 we find him reporting that the Post Office have largely extended the employment of female labour, and giving the grounds on which he considers their employment desirable:

> In the first place, they have in an eminent degree the quickness of eye and ear, and the delicacy of touch, which are essential qualifications of a good operator.
> In the second place, they take more kindly than men or boys do to sedentary employment, and are more patient during long confinement to one place.
> In the third place, the wages, which will draw male operators from but an inferior class of the community, will draw female operators from a superior class.
> Female operators thus drawn from a superior class will, as a rule, write better than the male clerks, and spell more correctly; and, where the staff is mixed, the female clerks will raise the tone of the whole staff.
> They are also less disposed than men to combine for the purpose of extorting higher wages, and this is by no means an unimportant matter.
> On one other ground it is especially desirable that we should extend the employment of women. Permanently established civil servants invariably expect their remuneration to increase

with their years of service, and they look for this increased remuneration even in the cases, necessarily very numerous, in which from the very nature of their employment they can be of no more use or value in the twentieth than in the fifth year of their service. . . . Women, however, will solve these difficulties for the department by retiring for the purpose of getting married as soon as they get the chance. It is true that we do not, as the companies did, punish marriage by dismissal. It is also true that we encourage married women to return to the service; but as a rule those who marry will retire, and those only will return whose married life is less fortunate and prosperous than they had hoped.

On the whole, it may be stated without fear of contradiction that, if we place an equal number of females and males on the same ascending scale of pay, the aggregate pay to the females will always be less than the aggregate pay to the males; that, within a certain range of duty, the work will be better done by the females than by the males, because the females will be drawn from a somewhat superior class; and further, that there will always be fewer females than males on the pension list.

With all these attractive reasons for employing women set out before the authorities, it was not surprising that the number of women employed increased with great rapidity, both in London and in the provinces, and that their sphere of work was widened. Duties of a clerical nature, for which previously they had been considered quite unsuitable, were now given to them.

Every telegram sent throughout the United Kingdom was forwarded to the General Post Office for examination. It was necessary, for example, to see that the number of words was reckoned correctly and the requisite stamps affixed. Errors were often detected, to which the attention of the defaulting officials had to be drawn. This work of

EARLY DAYS

watching and checking the transmission of telegrams from the district and sub-offices would, Mr. Scudamore considered, be the very thing for women. "The work, which consists chiefly of fault finding," he remarks, "is well within the capacity of the female staff and has been performed in a very satisfactory manner." The remark was shrewd, as it recognized at an early stage that conscientiousness is a characteristic of most women, and also that the power to find fault might prove an asset.

The formation of the Telegraph Clearing House Branch was entrusted to Mr. Chetwynd, a believer in women's work, and soon "forty ladies" were employed in his office under the direction of a superintendent.

It is an interesting fact that, whenever the question of introducing women into a new sphere of work is considered, juxtaposition with men in the same room has been raised as an objection—the fact that they live in the same house or meet in church or theatre is usually overlooked. Indeed, for many years departments put forward as their main objection to employing women the structural alterations in the office which they thought necessary. Mr. Scudamore, however, was an enlightened man, and faced this difficulty boldly. "From the first day of the transfer," he reports in 1872, "the department entered on the experiment of employing a mixed staff in the same room or rooms. It was considered to be a hazardous experiment, but we have never had reason to regret having tried it. I am satisfied that, where large numbers of persons are employed with full work and fair supervision, the admixture of the sexes involves no risk, but is on the contrary highly beneficial. It raises the tone of the male staff by confining them during many hours of the day to a decency of conversation and demeanour which is not always to be found where men alone are employed.

"And, further, it is a matter of experience with us that the male clerks are more willing to help the female clerks with their work than to help each other; and that on many occasions pressure of business is met and difficulty overcome through this willingness and cordial co-operation. . . . I trust to see the plan which we have tried with so much success extended wherever work suitable for females can be found."

Mr. Scudamore's desire was fulfilled, and much work was soon found for "females" in the Post Office. Indeed, from then on we find the employment of women figuring in the Reports of the Postmaster-General, although his references to the subject are always characterized by a sense of adventure.

It is with pleasure [he writes in 1873] that I have given my approval to the measures that have been proposed for increasing the employment of women in the Post Office; the first step in that direction having been taken by my predecessor, Lord Hartington, in relation to the telegraphs. How much remains to be done towards removing those artificial barriers which have hitherto shut out women from lucrative employment may be gathered from the fact that, on a late occasion, when it was announced, by advertisement, that there were twelve vacancies for junior counter-women, at wages from 14s. to 17s. a week, more than 1,200 candidates presented themselves; the very thoroughfare, as I am informed, in the neighbourhood of the office of the Civil Service Commissioners in Cannon Row having been for a time blocked up.

A year later he records that forty-six female clerks are

EARLY DAYS

now employed in the Returned Letter Office, and that the Controller reports very favourably on their work, being surprised at its excellence and the quantity they get through. This extension of the employment of women was the subject of careful consideration before the Civil Service Inquiry Commission (the Playfair Commission), which took evidence this year. The women were employed, as the Controller, Mr. G. R. Smith, explained to the Commissioners, in returning ordinary letters to the persons who wrote them, after they had been examined by the male officials to ensure that letters containing anything of value, or any obscene remarks, were not handed to them. The evidence given by Mr. Smith is of considerable interest as showing the nature and value of women's work at this date:

What general result have you found from the employment of female clerks there; has it been successful or otherwise ?—So far as it has gone I consider that it has been a perfect success. . . .

Do you find that they are both quick and accurate in the performance of the work ?—Very much so. They have completely surpassed my expectation in that matter; they are very accurate, and do a very fair quantity of work; and, in fact, more so than many of the males who have been employed on the same duty. . . .

Do you find the female clerks are as easily kept in discipline as the male clerks ?—Quite so. I have never had the slightest occasion to reprove any one of them. . . .

Is there any condition as to their being married ?—It appears not, because I have recently had a young woman sent to me who is married. What the consequence of that will be I do not know. I am getting rather alarmed.

I suppose that she might have leave of absence under certain circumstances ?—That would be a question when the time comes. I do not know that there is any immediate probability of it. . . .

WOMEN SERVANTS OF THE STATE

In fact, you are judiciously and cautiously extending their work?—Just so. We think that we shall ultimately succeed in getting them to do more of the work, but we must be cautious in the matter, because the questions arising in connection with it are so numerous. . . .

Is there much jealousy as to the employment of female clerks in your department?—There is some jealousy. I have not heard it so much expressed on the part of the clerks themselves who are doing actual clerical duties as on the part of the men who are doing a kind of intermediate duty, and who are a class termed "assistants." They do not like the females coming in at all.

They think that the females are placing their labour at a disadvantage?—Certainly.

After this cheering evidence it is interesting to have that given by Mr. Patrick Comyns, a first-class clerk in the same department.

So far as the female returners are concerned [he declares], as long as the work is simple and straightforward, the mere returning of a letter for instance, which involves merely copying the address from the inside to the official cover, they get through it; but at any time when tact, discrimination, or judgment is required, I find that they are perfectly at a loss in the matter.

Have you had any experience of them?—Yes, I have had the immediate superintendence, for some months, of the female returners in our office, and I find that that is the case.

May not a great deal of that arise from want of experience? Were they not only appointed last year?—No. I think that generally where women perform official duties, their minds are wanting in those respects; that they are timid to a certain extent, and will not act without applying to another person if there is anything out of the ordinary way. . . .

What sort of difficulties would they feel?—Such, for instance . . . as in returning letters bearing the signatures of bishops or peers.

And you do not find the same difficulty with the boys?—Not to the same extent; the boys have more tact.

What is your opinion as to boy clerks?—As far as my experience goes I think that they are far better adapted for returning letters than girls, as letters of a very objectionable nature sometimes fall into their hands. . . .

Would not the boys be as much corrupted as the girls?—I think not; I do not think that it is so objectionable in a boy, but it is a nice question after all. . . .

But your chief gives a very high opinion of it [the employment of female labour]—Yes, I am aware of that; but I am, however, not in favour of having a number of young women returning letters, because I think that it is demoralizing, and that it is not a proper atmosphere for young women to be in; but, at the same time, as long as the duty is simple and straightforward, they can get through their work very well, unless some difficulty arises.

How far women can and should be employed has always depended on the attitude of the man from whom the enquiry is made. In spite of Mr. Comyns's view, Mr. Chetwynd remained firm in his belief that women were useful in the Civil Service.

How long have you had experience of the employment of female clerks?—Since March 1871.

Have they performed the duties to your satisfaction?—They have performed the duties excellently; they leave nothing to be desired.

That is to say, both as regards intelligence and the care and accuracy with which they perform the duties?—With regard to all those points.

Have you ever found them deficient in courage, or in undertaking the responsibility which was required?—I have never found them deficient in necessary courage.

WOMEN SERVANTS OF THE STATE

How much does a lady get through in a certain time?—Exactly the same as a man.

But the pay of the ladies is different?—I think that their pay is too low. The department also thinks so, and it is under consideration to improve it. . . .

Fortunately also for the women whose work was under such close review, they had a strong protagonist in their superintendent, Mrs. Arundel Colliver, who was called to give evidence before the Commission together with Mr. Chetwynd. Both witnesses declared that their experience differed from that of Mr. Comyns, and that they had never found any lack of tact or discretion on the part of the women. "I have never found any want of judgment," added Mr. Chetwynd, "or fear of responsibility. . . . Every person there has been taught not only what the work means, but how to do it, and they have been encouraged; whereas I think it possible that in other cases they may have been rather discouraged, so that perhaps they may have been employed on that class of work under less favourable circumstances." Both these witnesses were also favourably impressed by the health of the women. The average absence in the Clearing House, according to Mr. Chetwynd, during the past year had been very little over six days, and the women were certainly not worse in this respect than the men.

Thus by 1874 women were well established in the Telegraph Clearing Office and the Returned Letter Office. The next stronghold was the Savings Bank, and this was stormed in 1875, when some forty "young ladies" were taken on, and were set to work on the newly introduced Daily Balance Section of the office. "The employment of women on duties of this character was very generally regarded in the Post Office as the agreeable fad of a few influential people," the opinion being held that it was beyond women's capacity to add and subtract figures, and that anything in the nature of a balance sheet would be quite outside their comprehension. The formation of a class of female clerks in the Savings Bank was therefore a daring venture. But the Postmaster-General was able to report that "although, in arithmetic at least, the standard of acquirement is high, the majority of the candidates succeeded in passing the examination." And the Controller of the Savings Bank later admitted that one of his "earliest official recollections was of the surprise which was created by the discovery that pretty girls were taking office work quite seriously and adding up figures without making mistakes."

The forty "young ladies" did not, however, receive a warm welcome from their men colleagues. "The Post Office Authorities," says the *Civilian* (the Post Office journal of those days), "have resolved to introduce a large number of female clerks into the department. Forty young ladies are shortly to be placed on the establishment of the Savings Bank office, notwithstanding the vigorous protest of the Controller, who, in common with the entire staff, feels the grievous dangers, moral and official, which are likely to follow the adoption of so extraordinary a course. The gentlemen in the office contemplate holding an indignation meeting to protest against the proposed action of the authorities."

Every attempt was made to prevent women extending their field of work, and we have a clerk making a solemn declaration before the Playfair Commission that, although women might do the lighter part of office work, there would be a difficulty in their writing cross-entry acknowledgments, because they have to be written "with heavy pressure by means of very hard pens and carbonic paper." A hard pen was apparently more difficult to wield than a scrubbing-brush. The authorities, however, stood firm, and this extraordinary action on their part took its course.

Fortunately for the women, among their number was an outstanding personality, Miss M. C. Smith, who entered the Post Office in October 1875. It is not too much to say that, from the day of her appointment, she showed that she was more than equal to her task, so that, when in a few months' time it was decided to add to the number of women and place them under a superintendent of their own sex, it was upon Miss Smith, then in her twenty-third year, that the choice of the authorities fell.

Miss Smith believed in her sex and set herself to prove that the experimental stage was over and that women were worthy of the best work which could be given them. In May 1876 she was appointed Lady Superintendent, with a staff of 64 women. In 1896 this staff had grown to 900, and when, in 1898, in connection with a representation made by her for an increase to the upper appointments of the Women's Establishment, the Lords of the Treasury arranged for a thorough investigation of her branch, the result was, that the Postmaster-General was informed that it was impossible to arrive at any other conclusion than that the Women's Division was admirably managed and that the work was done both well and economically.

In a later chapter a short biographical sketch of this early pioneer woman is given. Here, however, it is only necessary

EARLY DAYS

to say that it was fully recognized, and indeed publicly admitted, that it was her demonstration of what organization and training could do "with material once regarded as unpromising which contributed more than any other factor to extend the employment of women on clerical duties to other branches of the Post Office and to other departments of the Civil Service." With the appointment of Miss Smith there was no going back for women in the Post Office; their numbers grew rapidly and they were given more and more difficult duties.

Undoubtedly public opinion was becoming increasingly favourable to the employment of women in Government service. In September 1881 an interesting article appeared in the *Nineteenth Century* on "Women as Civil Servants," in which the writer speaks of the great and increasing demand for remunerative employment of women and the need for a frank discussion of their present position and future prospects as members of the working community. The *Quarterly Review* of January 1881 also contained an article on "Employment of Women in the Public Service." A few years previously Anthony Trollope, in *Good Words*, gave one of his delightful descriptions of "The Young Women at the London Telegraph Office," while, at a meeting of the Social Science Congress in Manchester in 1879, Mr. Cooke Taylor, in a paper on "Civil Service Appointments for Women," warmly advocated these appointments being thrown open to them.

In the 'seventies the openings for middle-class women in which they could earn a living were very few indeed. Educational facilities were not open to them to any great extent and vocational training was practically unheard of. The employment of women in the Post Office helped to solve the problem; indeed, the clerkships were utilized largely for the relief of women of the upper and middle classes.

The next great change to be recorded was in the method of recruitment. Up till now, in order to get a clerkship it was necessary for a woman to procure a nomination from some influential person and then pass an examination. In 1881, owing largely to Mr. Henry Fawcett, who was then Postmaster-General and who set his face against all forms of patronage, the appointments to women clerkships were thrown open to public competition, the age of entry being eighteen to twenty years. Naturally this led to some agitation and to that safety-valve, letters to *The Times*, but from then women in the Post Office, like men, gained their appointments by free and open competition.

The success which attended the employment of women in the Savings Bank Department, where their numbers continued to grow rapidly, and where they gradually came to perform work of a technical character, led to their employment in the Postal Order Branch, under the direction of the Comptroller and Accountant-General, when this branch was established in 1881. Indeed, the branch was largely staffed by women. Women were also introduced into the Money Order Office, which was later amalgamated with the Postal Order Branch under the title of the Money Order Department, and in 1904 the London Telephone Service was staffed by women clerks transferred from the other departments of the Post Office, who were merged with the staffs taken over with the National Telephone Company.

The news of the efficiency of the women clerks spread

EARLY DAYS

to other departments, and in 1899 the Board of Education applied to the Post Office for the services of some of their women clerks. Miss Smith, with that far-sightedness which never failed her, saw here new fields to conquer and sent to the Board some of her best clerical officers.

The Registrar-General's Office followed suit, later to be followed by the Public Trustee, when that office was established.

In 1912, in connection with the formation of the Women's Branch under the National Health Insurance Commission, Miss Smith's assistance was again sought, and women clerks were transferred from the Savings Bank to the newly formed office. Indeed, Miss Smith never refused new opportunities for women. She felt assured they could master whatever was offered them and in this way planned for the future.

The work of women in the Post Office was continually being weighed up by Commissions and Select Committees —the Ridley Commission (1888), the Hobhouse Committee (Select Committee on Post Office Servants, 1906–7), and the Holt Committee (Select Committee on Post Office Servants, 1912–13), all heard evidence and scrutinized the work of the women civil servants of those days—and as a result there was no decrease in the employment of women, but instead a steady increase in numbers, a widening in the scope of their work, and a gradual improvement in their status. Women had proved without doubt that they could render a service in the Post Office.

THE LOCAL GOVERNMENT BOARD

If a Royal Commission had been appointed in 1871 to decide what posts in the Civil Service were the least suitable for women, they would probably have selected the telegraph and postal services, and suggested that it would not be quite so unsuitable to employ them in the Local Government Board. This department had been created that year, and to it were transferred the powers and duties of the Poor Law Board, the Local Government Act Department of the Home Office, the General Register Office, and the Medical Department of the Privy Council. Accordingly, in the Local Government Board were included departments intimately concerned with the health and care of the community. Just at that time, in connection with Poor Law administration, a lively controversy was in progress on the relative merits of boarding out pauper children and dealing with them in large institutions. Indeed, the whole question of the care of the children of the State was exercising the minds of progressive philanthropists. That this might be a subject in which a woman official would be of service could hardly be denied. Fortunately Mr. James Stansfield, a "Victorian champion of sex equality," was made the President of the new department, and in 1873 he took the daring step of appointing a woman inspector in order that he might have the woman's point of view as to the result on girls of the education at pauper schools. The new inspector was Mrs. Nassau Senior, daughter-in-law of the economist and sister of the author of *Tom Brown's Schooldays*. From Stansfield's letters it is evident, as the historians Mr. and Mrs. J. L. Hammond have recorded, that the appointment of a woman to the staff was an unpopular innovation, and that Mrs. Senior needed all the encouragement that he could give her in an unfriendly atmosphere. Speaking of this long afterwards, Stansfield said: "I did the thing which they hated most. I imposed a woman upon them. I made a woman a Poor Law Inspector. . . . Before I left the office I made the appointment permanent so that they could only get rid of her upon abolition terms. . . . Many of the officials could not endure the appointment, and it was the greatest trial for them."

In the light of to-day it is somewhat surprising that it should have been unendurable to the men civil servants that a woman should be asked to visit workhouse schools and report on the effect on girls of the system of education. Mrs. Nassau Senior was careful to keep strictly within her province. "I have given my attention almost exclusively," she stated, "to questions affecting the physical, moral, and domestic training at the schools. I have not attempted to judge of the scholastic work, as I required all the time allowed me for looking into the matters on which I knew that you more especially desired the judgment of a woman." She produced a thorough and courageous report, showing the serious abuses which existed. This report was published in 1874, as an appendix to the third Annual Report of the Board, and special attention was drawn to it in the body of the Report.

Mr. Stansfield went out of office in 1874, and the Report, which was followed by a great controversy, fell into unsympathetic hands, but undoubtedly it influenced the trend of public opinion and much of the subsequent progress in dealing with the children of the State may be attributed to it.

Unfortunately the workhouse child soon lost her champion, and the men officials of the Local Government Board the woman who had been imposed on them. Mrs. Nassau Senior resigned owing to an illness which proved fatal in

WOMEN SERVANTS OF THE STATE

1877. *The Times* remarked, in recording her death, that she was "the first woman who ever obtained a high-salaried appointment among men and on the same terms in one of the most difficult departments of State." She goes down in history as a graceful and accomplished woman, generally loved for simplicity and sweetness of character. She was, however, something more; this first woman civil servant of the higher grades had vision and courage to a marked degree.

Her report encouraged the boarding-out system, and by 1885 more than a thousand children were thus dealt with under regulations laid down in the Boarding-out Order. This Order enabled children under Boards of Guardians to be transferred from Poor Law Schools to foster homes under the auspices of voluntary committees formed in rural areas. No woman official was, however, appointed in Mrs. Nassau Senior's position until November 1885, when Mr. Arthur Balfour, then President of the Local Government Board, followed, although more timidly, in Mr. Stansfield's footsteps, and appointed Miss M. H. Mason for one year as Inspector of Boarded-out Children. Curiously enough, early in 1886 Mr. Stansfield was back again in office as President of the Local Government Board, and it was he, therefore, who signed the Annual Report in which Miss Mason's appointment was announced.

Suggestions have on several occasions been made [runs the Report] as to the desirability of the inspection by a Lady Inspector of the children who are placed by the Guardians under the charge of boarding-out committees under the regulations referred to, and in November last we appointed Miss M. H. Mason as an Inspector for a limited period with the duty of

EARLY DAYS

visiting children so boarded out in different parts of the country, with the view of obtaining information as to their condition and of ascertaining whether our regulations are duly observed.

Miss Mason set to work on her investigations with great energy. Her reports, which give vivid pictures of the homes and conditions of life of the boarded-out child of those days, show that she covered much ground and enquired with meticulous care into every detail. After she had submitted two reports, approving the system of boarding-out if accompanied by thorough supervision, her appointment was extended, but her services were not made permanent until 1892.

In 1898, owing to the expansion of the work, it became necessary to appoint another woman inspector, to the satisfaction of Miss Mason, "not only," as she writes, "because the work has been far too much for me alone, but because of the recognition thus given to the fact that a woman alone can with propriety thoroughly inspect the personal condition of the children. The thorough inspection I have always bestowed upon the children has thus resulted not only, as I hope, in benefit to themselves, but in permanently establishing in this department of boarding-out an entire and complete system of supervision and official inspection by women." In 1901 a third inspector was appointed, Miss Mason becoming the Senior Inspector. For another nine years Miss Mason carried on her work with unabated zeal, until she retired in 1910 under the age limit, having completed twenty-five years' service.

In January of that year she reports: "This, my report for 1909, will be my twenty-fifth and my last before retirement. I have taken out with me, in order to teach them the methods of inspection, members of every committee whose work I have inspected and of all classes from Royalty to small farmers and tradespeople."

Miss Mason's work was known all over the country; the reports published year by year under her name in the reports of the Local Government Board were widely read and commented on in the Press. She influenced public opinion, and she rendered to the Poor Law child an inestimable service. Like Miss M. C. Smith, she was a strong personality and she never spared herself. She was not, however, a pioneer in trying to get the Civil Service open to women; she lacked Miss Smith's far-sightedness in this respect.

While Miss Mason was proving that the boarded-out child needed the oversight of a woman Government inspector, public opinion, largely owing to the work of Miss Twining and the Workhouse Nursing Association, was coming to the conclusion that the maladministration of workhouses, especially the sick wards, also called for the services of a woman inspector. This led to the appointment in 1897 of Miss Stansfield as Assistant Poor Law Inspector in the Metropolitan District. She carried on her work as the only woman on this side of the Poor Law Department of the Local Government Board for thirteen years, acting always in the capacity of an assistant to the general inspector. Practically no mention is made of her in the annual reports, and little is known of her influence or the part she played in Poor Law administration; indeed, she was overshadowed by her men colleagues, and yet, in view of the abuses existing in workhouse infirmaries, her services must have been greatly needed. In 1906, however, she was called to give evidence before the Royal Commission on the Poor Laws, and this evidence displayed a wide knowledge of the care and treatment of women and children in Poor Law institutions, even though, as she said, "her duties had never really been very clearly specified." Gradually it became more and more obvious to outside opinion that the services of women officials must be needed in the supervision of the care of the poor and infirm, and in 1910 four fully trained nurses were appointed as inspectors under the Local Government Board. Their duties were the inspection of the Children's Homes under Boards of Guardians, Certified Children's Homes, and the general administration of Poor Law institutions, especially the sick-wards of workhouses and the separate Poor Law infirmaries. In addition they helped to supervise the work of the Boarding-out Committees. Their position, however, was an anomalous one; they worked as assistants to the men general inspectors and were dependent on them for their work. Some of these made full use of the services of their women colleagues, others did not. Men officials who had been visiting these institutions for many years felt, perhaps not unnaturally, that they were quite capable of making a full inspection; they did not want the woman's point of view on conditions which they had considered to be satisfactory. Others, however, were glad to hand over some of the work to the women inspectors. Although the women's work was thus controlled by the general inspector of the district, on whose good will they had to depend for any work to reach them, Miss Stansfield was appointed, on Miss Mason's retirement, superintendent of the women inspectors, and their reports on institutions, etc., were in the first instance submitted to her. She was allowed to follow Miss Mason's example, and published a separate report in the main report of the Local Government Board. This, however, dealt chiefly with boarding-out, and little is recorded of the work of the other women inspectors except where it touched this question.

It does not require much imagination to realize that the position of the women inspectors was a difficult one, and, in comparison with the practice adopted in some of the other departments, the use made of them under the Local Government Board was disappointing. Still the calibre of these women was such that their work, hampered as it was in some directions, cannot have been without effect. Their standards were high, their knowledge extensive, and their desire to improve conditions, which indeed needed improving, was heartfelt.

Miss Stansfield retired in October 1918, and for some months her post was left in abeyance.

THE BOARD OF EDUCATION

In December 1839 the Rev. W. Allen and Mr. Tremendheere were appointed to be the first two Inspectors of Schools. In 1883, forty-four years later, the first woman inspector, Miss Emily Jones, was appointed, but she was designated a "Directress of Needlework." It was her duty to advise the department in all matters relating to needlework, which had been a compulsory subject of instruction for girls in elementary schools since the code of 1862, and accordingly subject to inspection. It is recorded that most of H.M. inspectors had treated needlework very seriously, and many took considerable pains to master the rudiments of sewing with their own hands. Indeed, a distinguished man inspector, who was charged by a headmistress with ignorance of the difficulties of buttonhole making, calmly sat down and worked a perfect buttonhole in a few minutes. The code of 1882 emphasized the importance of needlework, and it was gradually realized that the inspection of this subject might perhaps be entrusted to a woman, under the title of a "directress," not an inspector.

In many directions the 'seventies were an important decade in the new use made of the services of women, but perhaps nowhere so much as in the field of education. The work of Miss Beale and Miss Buss, and of the two earliest colleges for women, Queen's College and Bedford College, was bearing fruit. We have in 1869 the foundation of Girton College at Hitchin, followed by the opening of other University Colleges for women, and in 1878 the London University threw open its degrees to women. We have also the establishment of training colleges for women teachers in elementary schools and training colleges for domestic subjects. Contemporaneously with the sitting of the Royal Commission on Technical Instruction, which was appointed in 1881, but before their findings had been published, a movement in the direction of more practical instruction in the schools had been set on foot by a band of women who had been influential in the founding of training schools of cookery in various parts of the country. As a result of their representations, harmonizing as they did with the convictions of the Commission, cookery was introduced into the code of 1882 for public elementary schools.

Again, therefore, it became advisable for the Education Department to have the assistance of a woman, and an

Inspectress of Cookery and Laundrywork, Mrs. Harrison, was appointed in 1890 to help in the task of inspecting these subjects in the schools. The title of "directress" was now dropped and an important milestone was reached. The appointment of Mrs. Harrison was made on the ground that it had become necessary "to examine for certificates of qualifications for teaching cookery those candidates who had been unable to attend preliminary lectures and examinations at one of the existing centres and, in view of the rapid increase in the grants paid to public elementary schools, to ascertain whether the girls had been properly taught cookery."

For the first few years the appointments were on a temporary basis, but in 1894 Miss Jones's successor, the Hon. Mrs. Colborne, was placed on the permanent establishment of the department. A rapid development now took place in the teaching of cookery and laundrywork in elementary schools, and in 1898 it was decided that the department should themselves examine and grant certificates in cookery in the training schools. This new branch of work necessitated the appointment of Assistant Examiners, specialists in their subjects. Two women were appointed, and they made important recommendations to the Board as to the length of training and kind of syllabus advisable.

About this time also the needs of girls' and infants' departments in elementary schools came up for consideration, and four women were appointed in 1896 and 1897 as sub-inspectors to assist the men inspectors. It was indeed high time that infant schools should be visited by women understanding little children. In the *Report on Children under*

EARLY DAYS

Five Years of Age in Public Elementary Schools drawn up by them and published in 1905, we learn that in London the following was the usual time-table for infants of this age: "The morning devoted mainly to the Three R's, with a fourth lesson for singing, object-lesson or recitation. The afternoon divided between object-lessons, manual work, needlework, drills, singing or recitation, and further instruction in the Three R's. Kindergarten games once or twice a week and a short-story lesson on Friday afternoons." In this same report a picture is drawn of children of three and four years sitting at desks or on galleries for long periods at a stretch with no resting time, and being continually "talked at," the baby-teacher wearing out herself as well as her charges by this never-ending stream of instruction. The same inspectors found in their investigations that considerable value was attached to the religious knowledge of children under five; such a comment as "the babies' knowledge of the Holy Trinity left something to be desired" was found in the report of one of the diocesan inspectors. Indeed, the women inspectors had plenty of scope for their labours, and they undoubtedly laid the foundations for the well-equipped nursery schools and kindergartens of which we are now so justly proud. The number of women inspectors of elementary schools was gradually increased, and in 1903 there were six such women of the rank of junior inspector.

Thus, when Sir Robert Morant became Permanent Secretary to the Board of Education in that year, he found a few women inspectors, none of whom dealt with either elementary training colleges for women or with girls' secondary schools. Sir Robert Morant was a great administrator and he was also a great adventurer. It is said that he speedily made his influence felt in the utmost recesses of the Board, whether at Whitehall or in the country, and it was soon realized that a master-mind with vision and courage was in control. Undoubtedly the hall-mark of a man who is in the first-class rank of his particular job is the attitude he takes to a woman colleague. It is the man who is second-class at his work who opposes the entry of women into his province. Sir Robert Morant had always been a great believer in utilizing the services of women in work relating to women, and, although the situation was not without its difficulties, he set himself to develop a real woman inspectorate. The first step to be taken was to appoint a Chief Woman Inspector on whom would be placed a great responsibility, as on her would largely depend the success or failure of the movement. The choice fell on the Hon. Maude Lawrence, a member of a family renowned for its administrative ability and devoted service to the Empire. In 1905 she was appointed Chief Woman Inspector of the Board of Education. She was strongly supported by Sir Robert Morant and the Chief Inspector, Mr. F. H. B. Dale, and in this she was indeed fortunate.

"It was mainly owing," so one of her staff records, "to her tact and forceful personality that the establishment of a staff of women inspectors, competent to undertake the work of inspecting and advising on the training of girls and young children, as visualized by Morant, became a reality. This work had been previously done entirely by men. Though not an educationalist in the expert sense of the term, Miss Lawrence gave what was even more needed at that time, the whole force of her prestige and personality, to building up a woman inspectorate and to creating good relations between the men and women inspectors and between the Board and Local Authorities."

The first sign of the change was the improvement made in the status of women by admission to the rank of "His Majesty's Inspector" through Order in Council, although their salary scale was unaltered. The duties of women inspectors were thus defined in the Board's Report for 1904-5: "There are many matters that women alone can satisfactorily handle, and the Board believe that the steps they have taken in this connection will have many useful results.... Previous to 1903 there were six women junior inspectors for elementary schools, and one woman junior inspector attached to the Technological Branch of the Board. They were all subordinate officers of the men inspectors to whose district they were attached. These junior inspectorships for women have now been abolished and a staff of women inspectors created which now numbers eleven. They are organized under the Hon. Maude Lawrence, who was specially selected for this work.... Their duties will be to undertake inspection and enquiry into all matters specially needing the scrutiny and advice of a woman, and their work will not be limited to particular districts." This, then, was the charter of the women inspectorate granted by Sir Robert Morant.

One of Miss Lawrence's first recommendations for appointment was that of Miss I. A. Dickson, a student of Bedford College and graduate of Girton, who early made her mark as Inspector of Women's Training Colleges. Her appointment in 1905 was followed by that of two women Inspectors of Secondary Schools and also of several additional women Inspectors of Domestic Subjects. The Report of the Committee on Physical Deterioration had laid great stress upon the teaching of cookery in public elementary schools "as an important element in the well-being of the classes to which the children attending those schools belong." Accordingly the women inspectors paid special attention to this question, and in 1907 Miss Lawrence made a report on the subject which was the first comprehensive report ever submitted over the signature of the Chief Woman Inspector. In 1908 the first woman inspector of Physical Training was appointed, and in 1910 the women's training colleges, which had previously been allotted to the men inspectors (Miss Dickson accompanying them to inspect the domestic side), were entrusted to two women inspectors, who were made entirely responsible for them.

The woman inspectorate which Sir Robert Morant had set out to establish was thus growing rapidly both in numbers and scope of duties. He felt that the work of the Board was constantly touching matters in which men's knowledge and perceptions could not be entirely adequate or appropriate, and that in every branch of education of women and girls the woman's point of view was essential. How this necessary influence was to be brought to bear within a department largely composed of men in as harmonious a way as possible was the difficulty, a difficulty which has been experienced by all departments on the introduction of women into an inspectorate. Morant set out to devise machinery and procedure, and he laid down certain definite lines on which the woman inspectorate was to be organized. In view of the developments which have taken place in later years, Morant's organization is of considerable interest. As already recorded, a Chief Woman

EARLY DAYS

Inspector was appointed, and every woman inspector, whether she inspected training colleges, secondary schools, physical training, or domestic subjects, was a member of her staff. To emphasize this fact, the Chief Woman Inspector was responsible for selecting the particular woman for appointment by the President, and then for formally introducing her on appointment to the particular chief inspector in whose sphere her work would mainly lie. At that time there were Chief Inspectors of Training Colleges, of Secondary Schools and of Elementary Schools. With the exception of the Inspectors of Domestic Subjects, who reported directly to the Chief Woman Inspector, the daily work for each woman was mainly laid down for her by the chief inspector to whose branch she was delegated, and it was to him she directed her diaries of work. On the other hand, in various respects she was also under the Chief Woman Inspector, and it was to her she was told to look for advice and assistance if she experienced any difficulty which could not be removed by conference with the chief inspector. The Chief Woman Inspector was instructed to preserve close official relations with the various chief inspectors.

Perhaps in those early days some such organization was advisable, but undoubtedly it demanded tact and discretion on the part of all concerned if the arrangement was to be a harmonious one. If a conflict of opinion arose between a woman inspector and the inspector with whom she was working, it was laid down that she might directly consult the Chief Woman Inspector. Cumbersome as it seems in the light of to-day, the arrangement must have worked, for in 1909 we have a woman inspectorate consisting of a Chief Woman Inspector and twenty-seven women inspectors, and Sir Robert Morant saying that he was contemplating an increase in their number. The next years showed development, and we have the appointment of a number of women inspectors either of university standing or with valuable teaching experience. A few women were promoted to a higher scale, given after "long and meritorious service."

In those early days the men inspectors were in charge of districts arranged geographically, and in these districts they dealt directly with the Local Education Authorities and with the miscellaneous work which arose; they were alone responsible for the education in their area. The women inspectors, on the other hand, were specialists in connection with girls' education only and in this assisted the men inspectors. Thus the women inspectors were not gaining the experience which would allow them in time to become district inspectors. Still, by 1914 the woman inspectorate established by Morant had made good, and the services which they were allowed to render were appreciated.

It was not only in England that women inspectors for domestic economy subjects had been appointed. The Scottish Education Department and the National Education Board for Ireland both employed women for this purpose, the former also using specially qualified women occasionally to inspect girls' schools, paying them a fee according to the time occupied.

During these years also the women clerks who had been introduced into the Board of Education through the offices of Miss M. C. Smith of the Post Office were proving their worth, and by 1912 there were nineteen of them dealing with work that arose under the Teachers' Superannuation Act of 1898. The women were graded in a special class

EARLY DAYS

separate from the men and were known as Lady Clerks. If Miss Smith read the evidence given before the MacDonnell Commission in 1912 by Mr. L. A. Selby-Bigge, the Permanent Secretary of the Board of Education, she must have felt proud that the work of the women clerks whom she had sent to the Board was described as "all that could be desired," and that the officers of the Comptroller and Auditor-General's Department gave it a very high testimonial. That they were not employed only on simple work is clear, for it was described by one witness as "a very good class of second-division clerks' work."

The women clerks, however, were segregated from the men's staff; they worked in a watertight compartment, with practically no possibility of promotion. When Mr. Edmund Phipps, who appeared before the Commission with Mr. Selby-Bigge, was asked whether it would be possible "to organize a department in such a way that the best man or the best woman, the one or the other, should be appointed over each other's heads or alternatively according to seniority or ability," he replied that "it would not be possible to do so now," though "it might be in another generation if the way people look at these things changed."

No one who heard that reply contemplated a world war which made people look at things in a very changed way indeed. It did not require another generation to bring about the alteration in organization and outlook indicated in the question.

WOMEN SERVANTS OF THE STATE
THE BOARD OF TRADE

Although women were not employed to any large extent in the Board of Trade, their employment there and the circumstances leading up to it had wide and far-reaching repercussions.

Until 1886 no full and accurate labour statistics had been collected or published. In that year, on the motion of Charles Bradlaugh, the House of Commons passed a resolution deciding that in future these statistics should be collected. As a result a Labour Correspondent was appointed under the Board of Trade whose duty it was to collect statistics with regard to hours of labour, the conditions of the working classes, the state of the labour market, and similar matters, while the Statistical Department of the Board carried out the first attempt at a census of wages.

About this time also the attention of public opinion was becoming riveted on what was known as Sweating, the chief features of which were low wages, long hours, and insanitary surroundings. Undoubtedly the women workers were the chief sufferers under this system. Women's organizations, both political and social, took up the matter vigorously. The question was regularly on the agenda of their meetings, and resolutions were passed condemning it. At last in 1891 the turning point in the agitation came, and a Royal Commission on Labour was appointed, with the Duke of Devonshire as chairman. Mr. H. J. Mundella was appointed head of one of the groups into which the work in connection with the Commission was divided, and under him were appointed four women Assistant Commissioners, Miss Orme, Miss Collet, Miss Abraham and Miss Irwin, whose duty it was to investigate women's questions in

EARLY DAYS

connection with industry. The report presented by these first official women investigators of industrial conditions received high praise, and Mr. Geoffrey Drage, one of the two secretaries of the Royal Commission, furthered the movement by employing as clerks to the Commission university women, amongst whom was Miss Adelaide Anderson.

In 1893 Mr. Mundella was appointed President of the Board of Trade, and the work of collecting statistics and other information with regard to labour conditions was further developed, a separate branch known as the Labour Department being created for this purpose. The first head of the Labour Department, the "Commissioner for Labour," had under him three Labour Correspondents, one of whom was Miss Collet, who was to be specially concerned with women's industrial conditions. A monthly organ, the *Labour Gazette*, was started, to give up-to-date information as to employment, disputes, wages, etc., in the United Kingdom and other countries; important reports were also issued on changes in wages and hours of labour, unemployment, wholesale and retail prices, and other kindred subjects.

As women were being employed more and more in industry, problems of great variety and complexity were arising, and Miss Collet's work rapidly developed, so that she was allowed to have an assistant investigator. She chose a woman who had had a brilliant university career; she married, however, within two years and left the service. Miss Collet chose a second, a third, and finally indeed a fourth outstanding university woman with similar shattering results, and it was not until 1903, when she was appointed Senior Investigator for Women's Industries in the Commercial, Labour, and Statistical Departments of the Board of Trade, that she had the assistance of a woman who 'stayed the course.'

In spite of these changes, Sir Hubert Llewellyn Smith, Permanent Secretary to the Board of Trade, when giving evidence before the Royal Commission in 1912, stated that the women in the Labour Department were doing very important work, and that it could be extended, although he had to admit the loss to the department of the services of trained experts through marriage was a serious difficulty.

Still the women who remained carried on their investigations with zeal. Amongst other matters, they made a detailed enquiry into the cost of living of wage-earning women and girls and published a report on their findings. Although the employment of women on this specialized class of work was limited, it formed an excellent jumping-off ground. The Factory Department at the Home Office, the Ministry of Labour, the National Health Insurance Commission, all recruited women from this source; while Miss Collet herself, who was a recognized expert on statistics, was the first woman to be appointed to an important inside post of an administrative character.

In 1910 the first Labour Exchanges were set up by the Board of Trade, and Miss Collet's assistant was appointed as secretary of the committee for considering the staffing of the women's side of the exchanges. From the outset it was decided to employ women as well as men as clerks, and a number of women were appointed for registration duties and also for the more responsible duties of supervision. These appointments were at first made on a temporary basis, and the women selected were chosen on account of their knowledge of local industrial conditions or their qualifications as social workers. The appointments were open to existing established women civil servants, but, as the appointments were temporary, few could take the risk of applying for them. This proved a disappointment to some of the women employed in the Post Office, who had been longing for work which would bring them into closer touch with people who were in need and for whom they could perform a direct service. The Board of Trade was approached and as a result agreed to appoint a certain number of established women civil servants by transfer from the Post Office. There was also, in each of the divisional offices, a women's section, staffed entirely by women officers under a chief woman officer, who was responsible for the organization of the women's departments in the exchanges. These women were carefully chosen and were mostly university graduates. They brought to their work great devotion and never spared themselves in helping to shape and develop this new enterprise, with all its interesting possibilities of serving their fellow men. Unlike other departments, the men and women officials in the labour exchanges were recruited at the same time; there was not an existing men's staff on which women were "imposed." A new stage in the history of women in the Civil Service had been reached.

In spite of, or perhaps even because of, the Labour Department in the Board of Trade, the anti-sweating movement continued. This was a matter which could not be put right in a day, and public opinion was stirred afresh by the Sweated Industries Exhibition of 1906. Two years later a Departmental Committee on the Truck Acts was appointed by the Home Secretary, and the same year a Select Committee on Homework issued a valuable report. Low wages and their far-reaching results became one of the burning subjects of the day. Miss Collet's staff was employed in the task of collecting information as to the wages paid in these sweated industries, and made extensive enquiries into the lace, tailoring, chain, and embroidery trades, and outside pressure grew stronger. Finally the agitation was successful, and the year 1909 witnessed the passing of the Trade Boards Act, which provided for the payment by employers of a minimum rate of wages, clear of all deductions, in certain specified industries which were regarded as sweated trades. Until the creation of the Ministry of Labour this Act was administered by the Board of Trade, and a special Trade Boards Department was set up. Both men and women inspectors were appointed to enforce the regulations, the women from the first having equal opportunities with their men colleagues. In 1911 the passing of the National Insurance Act resulted in a scheme of Unemployment Insurance, the administration of which was entrusted to the branch of the Board of Trade which controlled the labour exchanges. This necessitated a large increase in the number of exchanges and accordingly more employment for women officials. In the same year a further administrative change was made by the formation of a department to concentrate on conciliation work, and the Chief Industrial Commissioner's Department was set up.

Hence by 1914 there was in the Board of Trade a small band of women civil servants engaged on work of a specialized nature in connection with wages and employment, some of which was to expand beyond all expectation.

EARLY DAYS

THE HOME OFFICE

On August 29th, 1833, the Royal Assent was given to the fourth of a long series of British Factory Acts. By section 17 the King was empowered to appoint under his sign manual four Inspectors of Factories—probably the most important step in the history of industrial legislation. In 1893, sixty years later, after much discussion and with considerable hesitation, the first two women inspectors were appointed.

As has already been said, the 'seventies was an important decade in the history of the progress of women. Even amongst the women in industry, those women who were accustomed to regard themselves as dependent and inferior, there was a movement towards raising their position. This movement was led by a woman trade unionist, Mrs. Emma Ann Paterson, to whom working women owe an eternal debt for her wise, practical, and incessant labours. She advocated the appointment of women as Inspectors of Factories, and in 1878, at the Bristol meeting of the Trades Union Congress, secured the passing of a resolution urging the Government to make such appointments. Three years later she arranged for a conference on the subject, at which Lord Shaftesbury presided. Public opinion was stirring on the matter, and the Chief Inspector of Factories became alarmed. Fortunately for him he was required to produce an annual report, which furnished him with a platform from which he could proclaim his views, and in 1879 we find him expressing himself at great length on the subject. "I doubt very much," he observes, "whether the office of factory inspector is one suitable for women. . . . In my last report . . . I gave some outline sketches of a day's work of an inspector. A perusal of these would force a

WOMEN SERVANTS OF THE STATE

conviction that it was the work for a man and not for a woman and that the general and multifarious duties of an inspector of factories would really be incompatible with the gentle and home-loving character of a woman. . . . Factory inspecting requires activity and acumen and the stern authority of a man to enforce obedience to his interrogatories. It is not an agreeable duty for a man, but I cannot conceive that such functions would commend themselves to a woman, or that she could successfully discharge them. I question the success of a female inspector in appearing at a metropolitan police court, conducting her case and having to submit herself in the witness-box to the cross-examination of an astute attorney. . . . It has been urged that where women are employed some enquiries could be more appropriately made by women . . . but it is seldom necessary to put a single question to a female, and I do not see how the services of ladies could be made available to render the administration of the laws more effective. Possibly some details here and there might be superintended by a female inspector, but, looking at what is required at the hands of an inspector, I fail to see the advantages likely to arise from her ministrations in a factory or a workshop, so opposite to the sphere of her good work in the hospital, the school or the home."

Still the agitation grew and pressure from various sides became stronger. The speeding up of machinery, the excessively long hours of work, the evils of bad sanitation, the alarming instances of lead poisoning, and excessive fines and deductions from uncertain wages, all told heavily on women workers, and it was felt unjust that women could not have one of their own sex to appeal to against such abuses.

EARLY DAYS

The question was debated frequently in Parliament. On June 9th, 1892, for instance, some members urged the appointment of women to inspect work-places where the majority of employees were women. "This is a matter which has commended itself to the judgment of a very considerable portion of the public," said Dr. Tanner, "and in which I am sure I am speaking in the name of the ladies of England, Ireland and Scotland. I think women ought to be inspected by women." The Home Secretary made a cautious reply. He thought the men inspectors would be opposed to the appointment of female inspectors. Still, it might be tried as an experiment, but the work was only fit for a woman of mature age.

But the turning-point in the movement had come. The Royal Commission on Labour had been appointed and was at work. As has already been recorded, four Women Assistant Commissioners, including Miss May Abraham, were appointed at an early stage in the proceedings; their report received high praise and conclusively supported the demand for the appointment of women inspectors. In January 1893, at a political meeting of the National Liberal Federation, Mr. Asquith, speaking as Home Secretary, promised an increased factory inspectorate, and added, "I hope I may be able at the same time to do something, it will not be much, to gratify the desires of our lady friends for female inspection." Accordingly, in the spring of that year, Miss May Abraham (now Mrs. H. J. Tennant) and Miss May Paterson, who had had valuable experience of labour questions in Scotland, became the first two women factory inspectors. Mr. Asquith was far from correct when he said "it will not be much." He appointed two women

WOMEN SERVANTS OF THE STATE

who brought to their work a high standard and great devotion, and he gave them a liberal starting-point and a wide field of activity. He realized that, when opening a new career to women, the future would depend on the choice of the first women to fill the posts, and he chose well. Indeed, he had done something to establish what proved, as the years went on, to be one of the greatest public services rendered by women.

From what has already been said in previous sections, it is obvious that the most important decision to be taken was that regarding the official status of the women in the inspectorate. There was a body of opinion which urged that they should be engaged solely as subordinate assistants to the men inspectors, "never to be called on to discharge the higher duties of the office." The higher official opinion was opposed to this view, and from the first the women were given all the powers and duties of an inspector in the field of women's trades. It was in this field that they were needed, and their work there was practically limitless. By this decision they were saved from the hampering necessity of working entirely under conditions and according to standards already prescribed. Instead they were allowed to serve both employers and women workers with a woman's quick intuitive understanding and special experience. It was made possible for them, as far as women's trades were concerned, to bring their own standards into play and to organize their work on the lines which they felt would make for efficiency, always with the impetus, the pressing needs of the women workers. Undoubtedly their difficulties were great. As the Home Secretary surmised in 1892, the men inspectors were opposed to the appointment of women. Indeed, in the

EARLY DAYS

evidence given before the Royal Commission on Labour there was an almost unanimous opinion expressed by men inspectors against their introduction. The women were thus obliged to meet prejudice and opposition from many (not all) of their men colleagues. Men civil servants have never had to meet this peculiar obstacle which women have always had to face. That, in spite of it, women have accomplished much speaks well for their tenacity, forbearance, and perhaps also for their sense of humour.

In spite of the opposition from their men colleagues, the number of women inspectors was soon increased, and in 1894 Miss Adelaide Anderson was appointed, to be followed shortly by Miss Rose Squire and others. Their work was repeatedly the subject of appreciation in Parliament and elsewhere. In 1896 Mr. Asquith declared in the House of Commons that he was quite satisfied from recent experience that a great many provisions of the Factory Act of 1895 could not be satisfactorily enforced except by female inspection. Sir Matthew White Ridley, the then Home Secretary, agreed that much good had been done in the interest of the female workers of the country by the appointment of these lady inspectors; while in 1898 Mr. McKenna, speaking from the Opposition benches, said, "We know the very high favour with which they are looked upon by the working classes." It was, however, not only the working classes who looked on them with favour. Mr. Theodore Taylor, speaking as a factory owner, in the debate on Home Office estimates in 1904, desired "to acknowledge the very great debt of gratitude which employers generally were under to the women inspectors. There were very many abuses which employers were not aware of until they were brought to light by women inspectors." He joined in "the strong request that the number should be largely increased . . . the adoption of this course would tend to the efficiency of factory labour." The point was made in debate that the women inspectors could bring themselves into close contact with the workers and obtain from them with greater spontaneity actual facts of the real duties of their lives and work, and that this freedom of communication resulted in much better administration of the law.

Indeed, it had become clear and beyond all doubt that the Chief Inspector of 1879 was wrong; factory inspecting was a service eminently suitable for women, and the public demanded their services with a persistence which could not be resisted.

The Chief Inspector of 1879 had been unable to envisage a woman inspector conducting her case in a metropolitan police court. It is an interesting fact, however, that it was in this realm that she soon made conspicuous headway. Her moral courage (an attribute of many women) stood her here in good stead, and her ability was recognized later by the writer of an article on "Women and the Courts" published in *The Justice of the Peace*. "As witnesses of professional or official status," he declared, "women have established themselves as in no wise inferior to men . . . those who have adventured into the courts . . . have not failed. That they were capable of conducting cases had been demonstrated for many years by the women inspectors of factories employed by the Home Office, who had invariably done their work in court so as to excite the admiration of all who enjoy seeing work well done. . . . Their undoubted efficiency showed that there

EARLY DAYS

was no reason at all why women should not grapple with legal difficulties just as well as men."

With their increase in numbers it became evident that some form of organization must be adopted, and in 1896 the five women inspectors were, in accordance with their own wish, formally constituted a branch of the Factory Department, under the superintendence of Miss May Abraham, subject of course, as all branches were, to control by the Chief Inspector. In May 1897, a year after marriage, Miss Abraham retired, and was succeeded by Miss Adelaide Anderson, who continued to hold the appointment until August 1921, the branch maintaining its high standard of efficiency and integrity under her guidance. During the decade before 1914 an important development in the women inspectorate took place. Senior posts were created, and, instead of being a peripatetic team working from London, the inspectors were required to reside in the most important industrial districts, where they were responsible for large areas and superintended a slowly growing staff of women which numbered twenty-one in all just before the Great War. They continued, moreover, to exercise equal powers with the men inspectors as far as women's trades were concerned. The annual reports of the women inspectors were until 1914 issued as a separate section over the signature of the head of their branch. Thus a clear history of the progress of their work is maintained, and in addition a vivid description of the life of the woman worker is recorded, often with sad details and humorous touches.

It is outside the scope of this book to describe at any length the details of the work performed by women civil servants. The work of the women factory inspectors has been dealt with by Dame Adelaide Anderson in her book, *Women in the Factory—An Administrative Adventure 1893–1921*. In the foreword to this book Lord Cave describes the history of the woman inspectorate as "a story worth the telling, for it is a chronicle of a steady and dogged campaign, a few defeats and many victories." He enumerates the adversaries to be met, all the ills which threaten the "factory girl"—poisoning by lead or phosphorus, insanitary workrooms, accidents from unsafe machinery, phthisis, anthrax, overstrain, truck and sweating, and more besides. "Readers," he concludes, "if their imagination serves them, may read between the lines stories of suffering, of endurance and of rescue, which will set them wondering why our predecessors so long grudged to the woman worker the help which only a woman can give." The woman factory inspector was always allowed to give this help, and Sir Edward Troup, Permanent Under-Secretary for the Home Office, admitted without hesitation before the MacDonnell Commission in 1912 that "the work of the women inspectors is of a character quite as important and as responsible as that of men inspectors."

But it was not only the women and children in our factories who were requiring the services of the woman official. Public opinion was stirring in regard to the needs of the delinquent child. In 1854, 14,000 juveniles passed through the prisons of England and Wales, of whom one-third came from London. Before the middle of the nineteenth century "the law recognized no difference between the adult and the juvenile—both were, or could be, treated alike—hanged, transported or imprisoned—with the following exceptions only; an infant under seven years of age was

EARLY DAYS

presumed to be incapable of committing a felony. As to children between seven and fourteen, although there was presumption against felonious intent, this was apt to be rebutted when deliberation was shown. A lad of ten, having killed and concealed the body of a companion, was held responsible, because it was assumed that he could discern good from evil—and he was consequently hanged."

Chiefly owing to the intervention and by the enterprise of private philanthropists, especially Mary Carpenter of Bristol, reformatory and industrial schools came into existence in the middle of the last century. To Mary Carpenter, as to Elizabeth Fry, the reform in the treatment of those in moral danger must be largely attributed. The first of these schools to be established had no connection with the State; they were independent institutions provided by charitable persons or societies for the reception of young offenders and neglected children. In 1854 an Act was passed empowering courts to commit young offenders to the reformatory schools, provided that they had been certified by the Secretary of State as fit for their reception, and empowering Treasury contributions to be made towards the maintenance of the inmates so committed. A somewhat similar Act applying to industrial schools was passed in 1857. These provisions necessitated the inspection by a state official. As, in 1835, an Act had been passed which had instituted Home Office inspection for prisons, it was perhaps not surprising that a prison inspector, the Rev. Sidney Turner, should have been charged with the inspection of the Certified Reformatory and Industrial Schools. He undertook this work single-handed from 1857 to 1868, when an assistant was appointed. From that time the staff was gradually increased, but the principal inspector of reformatory and industrial schools seems to have been appointed as an Inspector of Prisons until 1908, when the Children's Act of that year provided for the appointment of a special inspectorate. In December 1903 the Treasury approved the appointment of a woman inspector, designated a Lady Sub-Inspector, and in June 1904 Mrs. H. E. Harrison took up her duties as inspector of the girls' schools. In the Annual Report for 1907 reference is made to her work, and it is stated: "The reports will afford some idea of the ground that is covered and the progress that is being made in the training of the girls to become useful and intelligent women," and in the report for 1909 the Chief Inspector makes special acknowledgment of her assistance.

In 1911 a Departmental Committee on Reformatory and Industrial Schools was appointed, and in their report, published two years later, they recommended the appointment of an additional woman inspector. "At present the time of the one woman inspector is almost wholly occupied by the inspection of girls' schools, and it is only rarely and for some special reason that she visits any boys' schools. All boys' schools should occasionally be visited by a woman inspector as part of the regular routine of the department. A woman will often notice points seriously affecting the comfort and welfare of the children, especially points in connection with matters of domestic arrangement, that may escape the notice of a man. We think it would be a great advantage that this additional woman should be a qualified doctor." This recommendation was acted upon, and in 1914 a woman medical inspector was added to the staff.

EARLY DAYS

At the same time as the care of the delinquent child was attracting public attention, reformers were urgently pressing for improvements in local prisons, with the result that Government interference gradually increased. The Act of 1835, instituting Home Office inspection of prisons, was followed by further legislation of a tentative nature, leading up to the Prison Act of 1877, which transformed all local prisons into Government establishments, and constituted the Prison Commission, which, under the general control of the Home Secretary, carried on the whole prison administration.

In 1894 the Home Secretary, Mr. H. H. Asquith, appointed a departmental committee to enquire into prisons, with Mr. Herbert Gladstone as chairman, and a year later the committee issued a comprehensive report on prison administration. Amongst the questions to which they gave careful consideration was prison inspection, which they considered might with advantage be modified, as, although carried out with zeal, it assumed a somewhat formal and routine character. "We think it desirable," they report, "that a special arrangement should be made for the inspection of prisons, or those parts of prisons, assigned to women. A lady inspector appointed for this purpose alone would not be sufficiently employed, but we think that a lady superintendent might be appointed, who could not only do the ordinary work of inspection, but who could also be responsible for the general supervision of female prison industry and for such other duties as the Secretary of State might consider it desirable to assign to her."

The Prison Commissioners, to whom the recommendations made by the departmental committee were submitted for their observations, would have nothing to do with such a revolutionary proposal as this. "We are strongly in favour," they declare, "of the superintendence and visitation of female prisoners by philanthropic ladies, and we are of opinion that this recommendation may be adequately met by the extension of voluntary effort. Moreover if, as the Commissioners hope, it can be found possible to admit ladies to a larger degree to the work of Visiting Committees and Aid Societies, we think that the object aimed at by the committee would be so attained without cost to the State. We do not therefore feel justified in recommending the appointment of a salaried lady superintendent." The recommendation of the committee was therefore shelved.

In May 1907 the question of the appointment of a woman inspector was raised in the House of Commons in Committee of Supply by Mr. Pickersgill, member for Bethnal Green, who maintained that "the interests of women prisoners were prejudiced by the fact that there was not a member of their sex upon the higher executive of the Prisons Department. The members of the [Prison] Commission and the inspectors were all men. That seemed a little unfair and unreasonable when it was remembered that over 50,000 women passed through our prisons every year." He suggested that there should be a woman on the Commission and that there should be one woman among the inspectors, as many of the subjects dealt with by the latter fell within the domestic sphere and were more within the purview of women than of men. He was supported by Mr. Pike Pease, member for Darlington. In reply Mr. Herbert Gladstone, who was now Home Secretary, said he was not in favour of making a woman Prison Commissioner, but he thought the time had come when there ought to be some woman in a higher position of authority than that of chief matron. He took the necessary steps, with the result that in January 1908 the Treasury approved the appointment of a woman inspector, who was also to act as inspector of Inebriate Reformatories. A woman doctor was accordingly appointed in April 1908 to this post, which she held until 1921.

THE NATIONAL HEALTH INSURANCE COMMISSION

In 1911 the great scheme for National Health Insurance had been forced through Parliament in the face of opposition, and, when it finally passed the Commons with all its amendments and modifications, it was realized that to bring it into operation would indeed be a formidable task. Mr. Lloyd George, the sponsor of this great scheme, looked about him for a man who would be strong enough to tackle the task, and it was not surprising that his choice should fall on Sir Robert Morant, the civil servant who perhaps above all others possessed driving-force and vision. Accordingly on November 28th, 1911, Morant's appointment as Chairman of the National Health Insurance Commission for England was announced in the House. He was also to serve on the Joint Committee that was to form the connecting link between the Commissions of England, Wales, Scotland, and Ireland.

The first requirement was, of course, staff, and, after some months of bringing pressure to bear, Morant received the necessary authority enabling him to approach the heads of Government departments and obtain from them the transfer or loan of their most promising assistants. And he did not ask only for the transfer of men civil servants. He brought with him to the National Health Insurance Commission his belief in women's capacity and in women's powers of service, and so from the first we find women taking their share in bringing this great scheme for public health into operation.

Four women Insurance Commissioners were appointed to serve on the English, Scottish, Irish, and Welsh Commissions respectively, and received equal pay with their men colleagues, at what was then considered to be a fantastic salary for a woman, £1,000 a year. Women were recruited for all grades, some of the clerical sections being almost entirely staffed by women. In England the women inspectors were segregated, they were appointed to deal with women's trades, and the organization of the inspectorate of the Factory Department was more or less followed, the women officials working under their own woman head, subject to the Chief Inspector, and confining their work to the needs of women. In Scotland a more advanced policy was instituted, and there from the first men and women worked side by side and differences of sex were not recognized, the women inspectors dealing equally with men's and women's trades. That country was divided into six districts, and one of the districts was placed in charge of a woman inspector, with a staff of men and women under her. Indeed, we have here the first experiment of the system known as aggregation, a system of which more was to be heard as the years went on.

The value of the women's services soon received recognition. In a report on the administration of the National

EARLY DAYS

Health Insurance Act, reference was made to an important enquiry which the women inspectors had carried out and in which "they one and all gave evidence with extreme moderation, impartiality and discretion. The conspicuous fairness and success with which they had collected information were frequently a matter of commendation from employers."

THE SHORTHAND AND TYPING GRADES

A history of the early days of the employment of women in the Civil Service would be incomplete without reference to the typing grades. In view of the fact that there are to-day in these grades about 10,000 women, it is surprising to recall that, even as late as 1914, their number was estimated as approximately only 600. At the close of the last century the women thus employed were known as "female typewriters," a kind of "mechanical clerk," and it was some time before it was realized that they were indeed something more than a mere machine.

It appears that the Inland Revenue was the pioneer department in the employment of women as typists. In 1888 Sir Algernon Edward West informed the Ridley Commission that, though he himself was a very quick but very illegible writer, "these typewriting women can beat me two to one in writing, and that shows the amount of work that we get from them." These "typewriting women" took the place of "men copyists" and were particularly useful, so this witness said, for all important letters; for instance, "we correspond with the Treasury entirely by the typewriter." Sir Algernon West assured them that besides being quick the women were accurate and also very

WOMEN SERVANTS OF THE STATE

intelligent—they could even turn a letter from the third into the first person. Moreover, "they are cheap and there is no superannuation."

The actual machine was in its infancy and regarded by the Stationery Office as an innovation not to be greatly encouraged. The same witness explained that "there was now a new typewriter which had capital letters and that they were getting them by degrees."

In 1890 the Inland Revenue was not the only department to be sufficiently modern to make use of the services of women as typists; the Ridley Commission was informed by the Permanent Under-Secretary to the Foreign Office that they had one "lady typewriter," and that such an innovation worked "extremely well." Departments were still fearful of the consequences of employing men and girls in the same room. In the Board of Agriculture, according to Sir Francis Floud in his book in the Whitehall series, the one woman typist was secluded in a dingy little room in the basement, and the chief clerk issued an imperative order that no member of the staff over the age of fifteen was to enter her room.

Another department, which even to-day is shy of using the services of women, was brought to make the bold experiment of employing them, by receiving in 1889 a letter in the following terms from a high official in a neighbouring department. "We are delighted here with the type-writing . . . I had a separate room and convenience fitted up which would leave the ladies completely to themselves and free from any danger of interference. We have got two young women at (I think) 23s. and 21s. a week and they do their work excellently. I think they turn out as much work as four copyists could do. . . . We take a second pressed

EARLY DAYS

flimsy from the letter which they write. . . . The women are excellent and give no trouble." This letter encouraged the nervous department to engage in 1890 two "female typewriter copyists" in place of three men copyists (who had cost £100 a year each). They were supplied, to begin with, by the firm which furnished the typing machines and were apparently regarded as part of the machinery. Great care was taken to protect them. They worked in a locked room in the upper part of the building and their work and meals were served to them through a hatch in the wall. They left a quarter of an hour before the men, and no man was allowed to take work up to them without a special permit from a responsible official—only granted with great difficulty. The only time when they were let loose in the office was when they went to draw pay, and even then, in the early days, and as their number increased, they are said to have been marshalled in a crocodile by the Superintendent. All this, of course, made them intensely interesting to the men, who used to hide behind the pillars in the corridor to see them pass. Some difficulty was experienced, at first, as to the title to be given to these new officers; the suggestion was made that they should be called just "typewriters," so that their sex might not be disclosed, and a notice saying "To the typewriters" was put up at the foot of one of the upper staircases.

By 1892 we have women typists employed in at least seven departments; it would appear that the "female typewriter" had come to stay. They were not, however, themselves quite satisfied with being "cheap and without superannuation," and so My Lords of the Treasury were soon the recipients of a petition from the women typists, asking that their rates of pay might be increased, and that they might be placed on the permanent staff of the Civil Service, and a question was asked about their conditions of service in Parliament. As a result the remuneration and conditions of service of women typists were dealt with in a Treasury Minute of March 17th, 1894, and from that time women typists in effect became a class common to the service. It was not thought, however, that the amount of typing required would be great, and the Treasury did not anticipate that the number of typists would ever exceed a hundred.

From that time their numbers gradually increased, so that by 1914 there were about 600 women typists employed in about half the public departments, divided into two grades, typists and shorthand-typists, and working under the supervision of their own female officers. Although they now constituted a "class," different principles of recruitment prevailed in different departments. For the General Post Office and the Inland Revenue Department an open competitive examination was adopted; other departments nominated their typists, some singly for single vacancies, some in numbers exceeding the number of vacancies, and submitted them to the Civil Service Commission for an examination in a few simple subjects.

There was never really any doubt that in typing and shorthand women could render valuable service. Already, however, the typist staff had begun to make demands for admission to other ranks of the Civil Service, and, in giving evidence before the MacDonnell Commission, their representative stated that the typists felt the need for a wider outlet. They considered that the prospects of promotion were poor and that they should have the same chance as boy

EARLY DAYS

clerks of passing on into other classes of the public service. The "female typewriter" was beginning to feel, and to wish It publicly known, that she was not only a machine.

THE ROYAL COMMISSION ON THE CIVIL SERVICE, 1912–15

It is evident from what has already been said that, during the last thirty years of the nineteenth century, women civil servants rendered, as far as they were allowed to, a real service to the public. The beginning of the twentieth century found them eager for more scope and further opportunities for service. Hence they pursued a campaign by means of memorials and deputations to heads of departments and, though voteless, by representations to Members of Parliament. In 1910 Sir Charles McLaren, always a believer in women's powers, introduced a Bill into the House designed to secure equality between men and women civil servants. The Bill was backed by Mr. Philip Snowden and others, but on the whole received little support. Still, public opinion on the subject was growing, and it was therefore natural that, when the Royal Commission on the Civil Service was appointed in 1912, "one of the most important questions" which engaged their attention was concerned with "the conditions under which women should be employed in the service."

The evidence given before the Commission was practically unanimous as to the efficiency of the women's work. Whether their services were to be extended was a different proposition. Sir Robert Chalmers, Permanent Secretary to the Treasury, for instance, admitted that women had done very well indeed in the spheres in which they had been occupied, and that there was not a single case where the

WOMEN SERVANTS OF THE STATE

State had retraced its steps after appointing women to positions in the public service, or where the experiment had proved a failure. But he was afraid of "outmarching public opinion," he would prefer in this matter to follow, rather than lead, it. On the other hand, the Rt. Hon. A. H. Dyke Acland, Chairman of the Consultative Committee of the Board of Education, considered the aspirations of young women to enter the Civil Service on the same terms as men as "quite justifiable;" while Viscount Haldane, Secretary for War, declared: "My belief is that the exclusion of women from a great many professions at the present time is the result of superstition and very little else. . . . There are certainly a great many positions in the Civil Service which women can fill quite as well as men . . . higher division posts as well as others."

The old difficulty as to the employment of men and women together was frequently put forward. Thus Mr. Stanley Leathes, First Civil Service Commissioner, considered that to admit women to all the Civil Service examinations was a *very* revolutionary proposal. "I am not jealous of women," he explained, "but I think it would be rather awkward to have men and women working together shoulder to shoulder in the same department. I do not wish to see it. If we think of employing women, we always think—Is there a room where we can put them by themselves? If you can do that, there is a lot of work they can do very well. I do not wish to keep women out, but I think it would be very difficult to have men and women working side by side."

Mr. L. A. Selby-Bigge, Permanent Secretary of the Board of Education, while highly commending the work done by the women clerks, which he described as excellent, anticipated that difficulties would arise in the common employment of men and women, "difficulties of discipline, supervision, and promotion, and all the considerations that those terms involve."

This view was not, however, universally shared. The evidence given by Sir E. W. D. Ward, Secretary to the Army Council and Permanent Under-Secretary of State, is of interest. When asked: "Do you think there would be any prejudice to women working with men in some cases?" he replied, "For eleven years I have been trying to segregate the sexes. You still think it is necessary? The ladies at the War Office think they would like to be mixed up in their work more with the men. Does the head lady you are talking of think so? Yes, she thinks they both work better. I pointed out reasons against it, but she overpowered me."

Although it is obvious that the evidence was of a varying nature, there was one point on which the witnesses were agreed, namely, that the services rendered by the women were efficient. How were these services to be used in the future? The answer, as always, when women's work is under consideration, depends on how the man who has to make the decision estimates himself.

The conclusions of the Commission as to the employment of women were not unanimous. Not only did the Majority and Minority Reports differ on this point, but there were two reservations to the former.

This report began by showing the extent to which women were employed in the Civil Service generally in 1914. In the General Post Office there were about 3,000

WOMEN SERVANTS OF THE STATE

women and girl clerks, while in the Board of Education there were nineteen, in the Registrar-General's office two, and in the Public Trustee office seventy, but these latter were unestablished. In the typing grades about 600 were employed. In the Labour Exchanges and National Health Insurance Commission there were a number of women clerks, but no regular system of recruitment. There were 146 women inspectors in the Inspectorates and forty organizing officers in the Labour Exchanges and a certain number of women in important posts, e.g. women Health Insurance Commissioners and women employed by the Board of Trade on investigations connected with industries.

The majority laid down as their guiding principle that "the object should be, not to provide employment for women as such, but to secure for the State the advantages of the services of women wherever those services will best promote its interests." It was little thought then that the State would soon be in dire need of the services of all available women.

They could not accept the contention that justice required that, in recruiting the public service, the difference of sex should be ignored, as the evidence showed that "in power of sustained work, in the continuity of service, and in adaptability to varying service conditions, the advantage lies with the men" (a view which was soon to be changed by the World War). On the other hand, they considered that the work of women in the public service was most likely to be of value in activities connected with the interests of women themselves and of children, and they could not regard the employment of so small a number as forty-three women inspectors under three Boards of Education in the three

EARLY DAYS

Kingdoms, eleven under the three Local Government Boards, eighteen under the Home Department, and one under the Prisons Department, as sufficient for the "full discharge of duties of such grave importance." Further, they thought that women should be eligible for appointment to the staffs of museums and libraries.

In regard to the administrative grade they considered that specially qualified women should be eligible for appointment to particular posts and should be chosen by special methods of selection; they did not recommend the admission of women to these posts by competitive examinations as was the case for men civil servants. As to the clerks, they failed to understand why nearly 3,000 women were employed in the General Post Office and only about 500 in the rest of the public service.

They concluded by recommending that the Treasury, "acting in communication with the various heads of departments and after consultation with competent women advisors, should institute an enquiry into the situations in each department which might with advantage to the public service be filled by qualified women."

The signatories to the reservations to the Majority Report recorded their dissent to the statement that the evidence "shows that in power of sustained work, in the continuity of service and in adaptability to varying service conditions the advantage lies with men." They pointed out that efficiency depends in part upon the food, housing, recreation, etc., made possible by the salary paid; hence no fair inference as to the relative efficiency of men and women could be drawn from the work of existing women clerks, who were paid much less than male clerks. And as regards the women's adaptability, the statement was not justified even under existing conditions, being based largely on *a priori* considerations rather than actual experience.

They considered that in time the administrative examination should be opened to women and a limited number of places assigned to them. Any other form of admission might lead to the inference that women found their way into administrative posts more easily than men. The precluding of women from competing in the ordinary way could not be regarded as satisfactory or just. They were also of the opinion that the staff of the Treasury should include a woman to advise on matters affecting the organization of women in the service.

The Minority Report, while declaring that women as a class had no inherent right to state employment, any more than had any particular class of men—"with all alike it is a question of fitness rather than of right between class and class or between sex and sex"—favoured the extension of the employment of women in the upper ranks of the service, though to a lesser extent than in the lower ranks. They doubted, however, whether the intermediate ranks of the service, the lower administrative and upper clerical branches, presented a field in which at that time female labour could be usefully or conveniently employed.

It is evident that on April 2nd, 1914, the day on which the Fourth Report of the Royal Commission was signed, there was no definite policy or clear-cut view as to the future employment of women in the Civil Service. Any consideration of such recommendations as were made was prevented by the outbreak of the Great War.

CHAPTER 2

THE YEARS OF THE WAR

IN 1914 the employment of women in the Civil Service was limited. There was no interchangeability between women and men, and, speaking generally, women were restricted to special women's establishments and worked in watertight compartments. It was estimated that on the outbreak of war the total number employed was in the neighbourhood of 65,000, of whom 58,000 were in the Post Office non-clerical grades. In July 1919 the total had risen to nearly 170,000, and women were employed in all departments and on work interchangeable with men.

The reasons for this remarkable change were obvious. The recruitment of men to the established grades of the Civil Service was almost completely suspended, and men civil servants were volunteering and being called up for military service in large numbers. The staffs in the Service Departments were rapidly increased. Other existing departments, in particular the Board of Agriculture, were called on to take up new duties vital to the nation. New ministries had to be formed to cope with the new responsibilities which now faced the Government. The Ministries of Munitions, Food, and Pensions, the National Service, and the War Savings Departments, all came into being, and from all sides there was a demand for staff.

What would have been the position of women in the Civil Service in those early days, if the Great War had been anticipated, it is difficult to gauge, but it is probable that there would have been many more trained to take the place of men than proved to be the case. It was in the clerical classes that extensive use was immediately made of their services. The War Office, which had previously employed women to a limited extent, now recruited them in large numbers, on a temporary basis, and other departments rapidly followed suit. The woman typist also came to be freely employed. A certain reluctance was exhibited, however, in making use of women in the higher ranks of the services, and it was argued, perhaps not unnaturally, that the task of training recruits in work of an administrative or technical nature only added to the burden of an overworked staff.

It is true that the women of the nation were invited by the Government in the spring of 1915 to register for war service and that 80,000 responded. At the same time the Federation of University Women compiled a classified catalogue of trained women graduates, many of whom by reason of the stoppage of their normal labour were free for employment. But the use made of their services was at first very limited. A report drawn up for the meeting of the British Association in September 1915 by a committee of men and women well known in the field of labour research recorded the appointment of a woman in the Civil Service Commission in place of a first division clerk, of an additional woman factory inspector, and of language experts at the War Office, apparently the most noteworthy cases of substitution which had taken place. The compilers of the report observed that "the traditions of the service are wholly against the inclusion of women" in the higher branches of the Civil Service, "and the mere prejudice against [their] employment" in such posts "often biases and distorts the judgment."

At the annual conference of the Association of Headmistresses in 1915 a resolution was carried unanimously, "that this Conference regards the admission of specially qualified women to higher administrative posts in the Civil Service as urgently necessary to the welfare of the nation in view of the situation created by the war," and a petition on the subject was presented to the Government signed by a hundred and fifty men and women.

Meanwhile the situation was continually changing, fresh developments were rapidly occurring, and, with the growing realization that the war was not likely to be over in a few months, more and more men were volunteering for military service. The formation of the Auxiliary Women's Services, the Women's Army Auxiliary Corps, the Women's Royal Naval Service, and the Women's Royal Air Force Service, all gave impetus to the movement, as it became clear that women could do administrative work if given the opportunity. The services of women were now accepted as "promoting the public interest"—the criterion of the MacDonnell Commission—and it became the policy of the Government to consider the whole field of women's employment.

Accordingly women came to be entrusted, though on a temporary basis, with every kind of administrative, executive and clerical work, and with the supervision and training of staff, the Treasury agreeing to the enrolment of women university graduates as junior administrative assistants, and to the transfer of a few women from departmental to administrative work.

WOMEN SERVANTS OF THE STATE

In connection with the latter departure, women inspectors were employed in the Board of Education as examiners on the responsible work of examining into the grants to be made to schools and authorizing their payment. They also undertook other administrative duties of an important nature, and Miss Dickson was appointed an Assistant Secretary, a post she held until her death in 1922.

Hence university women were gradually employed on work equal to that done by junior higher divisional clerks or senior second divisional clerks. In this capacity they were found in the Board of Agriculture, the Foreign Office, the War Office, the Admiralty, the Air Ministry and other departments. They were often employed as private secretaries to higher officials, or as officers in charge of registries and records, and on these duties they worked in the India Office, the National Service Department, the Stationery Office, and the Board of Control.

In the Factory Department of the Home Office a number of temporary women inspectors were appointed, while the scope of the work of the permanent women inspectors was widened; they undertook duties in connection with men's trades and advised on the substitution of women for men in industry.

In the War Office much responsible work was given over to women. They had to draft letters and prepare decisions that would bind the department, and they had to exercise their own judgment to a considerable extent. They were employed on responsible accounting work, in army pay offices, in investigating disputes in connection with War Office contracts, and in coding and decoding telegrams.

In many departments they were used as translators, their

knowledge of foreign languages proving an asset. In Postal Censorship, so well did women acquit themselves that it became possible to release all men of military age who were fit. They rapidly learnt new languages and were found to be quick and discreet and to take their work very seriously. It was realized, to the surprise of some of their men colleagues, that women could keep a secret and did not divulge confidential information.

In the Board of Agriculture a number of women officials were appointed to encourage the employment of women on the land and to ensure an increase in food production. A women's branch was established, which administered the Women's Land Army, and the farmers had to resign themselves, often quite willingly, to discussing agricultural subjects with women organizers sent out by the Board.

The Labour Department of the Board of Trade—later the Ministry of Labour—was disposed to utilize women freely on responsible work. They employed a number of women officials, rapidly extended the employment exchanges, and dealt as best they could with the ever-increasing demand for women workers. The women officials took a large share in inaugurating training schemes for new processes, in the transference of workers, and in establishing advisory employment committees. In 1916 a post of Chief Inspector of Women's Employment, carrying a salary of £700, was created and a woman was appointed to it. A year later a woman was appointed as an Assistant Industrial Commissioner in the Chief Industrial Commissioner's Department of the Ministry of Labour, her work being that of conciliation in connection with trade disputes.

The Customs and Excise Department, entrusted with the

WOMEN SERVANTS OF THE STATE

duty of investigating claims to separation allowances made by sailors' and soldiers' dependants, largely utilized the services of women, both on this work and also on the administration of the Old Age Pensions Acts; and the Ministry of Pensions used women on every conceivable duty. Intelligence branches found them especially useful, and Government libraries were forced to open their doors to the woman university graduate.

In the Post Office women found their way into the branches of the work previously staffed by men. Sir Evelyn Murray records: "The employment of women was gradually extended, not without misgivings, to duties for which either from lack of experience or on grounds of physique women had previously been considered unsuitable. Each successful experiment led to others, and by the end of the war women were employed in large numbers both on day and night shifts as postwomen and on sorting duties, and even on work requiring considerable physical stamina, such as driving mail vans and repairing overhead telegraph wires."

The new departments made fuller use of their services. The Ministry of Food employed about a hundred university women as junior administrative assistants on definite administrative work and on statistical, accounting, and intelligence duties. Women became secretaries to committees and deputies to assistant secretaries in charge of divisions.

The new War Savings Department appointed women to deal with the advertising and designing work in connection with their schemes for publicity.

The Ministry of Munitions employed a large number of women and made great use of them even on the technical

THE YEARS OF THE WAR

side. They became inspectors of optical munitions, and technical assistants in chemical warfare, and undertook aeronautical and other research work. The woman chemist and physicist was much in demand. A number of women inspectors were also appointed to advise on and supervise the employment of women in government and controlled factories. In fact the munition factories became accustomed to dealing with the woman official on every kind of subject.

For all this work departments carried on their own recruitment, and women found their way into the Civil Service through every conceivable channel, especially in the early years of the war. There was no time for careful selection of candidates and efficient training, and no concerted use was made of women in the established staff as trainers and supervisors of the temporary staff.

No picture of the employment of women in the Civil Service during the war would be complete without reference to the girl messengers who, in their brown overalls, flooded Government Departments and did their best, often with considerable success, to cope with work formerly done by hoary-headed old men now promoted to other duties.

Indeed, by the end of the war the employment of women in the Civil Service was extensive, and men had become accustomed to them. They were engaged on every kind of work, sitting in the same room with men and even at the same table, supervised now by a man and now by a woman according to suitability; and these surprising changes were to be found, not only in the new departments, but also in the old-established offices of Whitehall.

Segregation of the sexes had been discarded by force of circumstances, and it was realized that the State needed both men and women working in harmony together. The extension of women's employment came to be regarded as of real interest to the country, and Mr. Asquith was only voicing the view of many when he said in 1917, in a foreword to *Women of the War*, by Miss Barbara McLaren, that it could not "be doubted that these experiences and achievements will, when the war is over, have a permanent effect upon both the statesman's and the economist's conception of the powers and functions of women in the reconstructed world."

The practical consideration, however, for civil servants was, on what conditions should women be employed in the services in this reconstructed world. Accordingly, towards the close of the war no less than four committees were set up to consider amongst other matters various aspects of the work done by women in Government departments. Their findings are of considerable interest. They all reported within the period December 14th, 1918, to April 30th, 1919, but on somewhat different lines. The two most important for our purpose were the Committee on the Machinery of Government, under the chairmanship of Lord Haldane, and the Committee on Recruitment for the Civil Service after the War, of which Lord Gladstone was chairman.

The Machinery of Government Committee, which was appointed to advise "in what manner the exercise and distribution by the Government of its functions should be improved," reported that they were "strongly of opinion that among the changes that should be made, as conducive to this end, must certainly be included an extension of the range and variety of the duties entrusted to women in the

Civil Service and in practically all departments." In discussing the question as to whether the Class I examination should be opened to women, they declared: "The practical question whether women can be found suitable to perform duties comparable with those assigned to men in Class I has to a large extent found an answer in the experience of the last four years, which has gone far to resolve any doubts upon the point.... We therefore think that it is no longer expedient in the public interest to exclude women on the ground of sex from situations usually entered by the Class I examination or from other situations usually entered by competition." There were certain posts in the Higher Division and in other grades for which, they held, women, if properly qualified, were *prima facie* more suitable than men, these posts should be assigned to women, and as regards other posts the "test of eligibility should have no relation to the question of sex." They stated their conviction "that the absence of any substantial recourse to the services of women in the administrative staffs of departments, and still more in their intelligence branches . . . has in the past deprived the public service of a vast store of knowledge, experience and fresh ideas, some of which would for particular purposes have been far more valuable and relevant than those of even the ablest of the men of the Civil Service."

Four months later the Gladstone Committee presented their report. Presumably they had been taking evidence at the same time as the Haldane Committee, but their findings were of a different nature. They expressed the view that relatively very few women had been engaged on general administrative work (this view being in direct contradiction to that implied in the report of the earlier Committee). The evidence as to the relative output of men and women, they stated, varied considerably, but it was generally agreed that women did not stand either a sudden or a prolonged strain so well as men. The amount of sick leave required by women was greater and the rate of wastage was also higher in the case of women, owing chiefly to marriage. The evidence did not favour competition between girls and boys and was indecisive as to segregation. "Neither the experience of temporary departments nor the experience of business houses is sufficient to decide whether it would be conducive to efficiency in permanent departments to place men under the control of women."

Their general conclusion was that it would be unsafe to introduce women forthwith as interchangeable with men throughout the various departments, and that a readjustment of this kind would require to be worked out by gradual processes and carefully tested stage by stage. The recruitment of women should be extended, but it should remain on separate lines, at least until further experience had been gained. The time had not come for throwing open Class I to women, but the experiment should be tried on a liberal scale of employing women in posts of a Class I type where the work was specially suited to them. "There is not sufficient proof," they added, "that women are at present capable of performing with equal efficiency the most responsible duties assigned to men, except in certain branches for which they are specially qualified."

Experience has shown that many of the fears expressed in this report were groundless, and even in 1919 public opinion was in advance of these cautious recommendations.

THE YEARS OF THE WAR

Two months previous to the presentation of this report had appeared that of the Committee on the Organization and Staffing of Government Offices, under the chairmanship of Lord Bradbury. One of their findings is of considerable interest. "In view of the fact that the experience of the war will probably result in an extension of the employment of women in permanent departments," they declared, "we recommend that the proposed Establishment Division of the Treasury should include one or more women officers, not so much to control the work of women as such (which in our opinion should not be dealt with on different lines to the men), but to take part generally in the work of the branch."

It took some years before the soundness and wisdom of this opinion was realized and the recommendation put into full operation.

The fourth committee was the War Cabinet Committee on Women in Industry, under the chairmanship of Lord Justice Atkin, which reported in April 1919. This report dealt only to a minor degree with women in the Civil Service, and in this connection chiefly with the question of equal pay for equal work. They recommended, however, that the separate grades and separate examinations for women clerks in the Civil Service should be abolished, the Government Departments retaining within their discretion the proportion of women to be employed in any branch or grade.

The debatable question of the employment of women in the service had thus engaged the attention of many trained minds, and once more there was a diversity of opinion on the subject. Still the fact remained, women had been tested in the service during the war in great numbers. Their recruitment had been haphazard, their training inadequate, and they had been required to undertake duties which had formerly been performed by men of considerable experience. Yet, speaking generally, they had made good. On all sides it was acknowledged that their work had been efficient. Even the cautious Gladstone Committee were of the opinion and ventured to recommend that the position of women in the Civil Service should be improved and strengthened. Indeed on May 19th, 1920, it was said in the House of Commons, "one of the great blessings of the war has been to show the value to the State of the services of women."

CHAPTER 3

POST-WAR SETTLEMENT AND
REORGANIZATION

HOW exactly these services were in future to be made full use of, what were to be the general principles which should govern the employment of women in the Civil Service, was the next question for consideration, and it was one over which considerable discussion took place during the years 1919 to 1921. It was obvious after the experience of the work of women during the war that fuller use must be made of them and that they must be given greater opportunities. Also they had become enfranchised, and this brought far-reaching consequences. On the other hand, drastic reductions in the staffs of departments had to be made and the ex-service man provided for.

The first move was the introduction by the Labour Party (on a private members' day) of the Emancipation Bill, which made women eligible for admission to all branches of the Civil Service. This Bill passed the House of Commons but was defeated in the Lords.

The Government then introduced its own Bill, the Sex Disqualification (Removal) Bill, and this was passed on December 29th, 1919. This provided that a person shall not be disqualified by sex or marriage from the exercise of any public function or from holding any civil or judicial office or carrying on any civil profession or vocation. But there was an important proviso, which ran as follows: "Notwithstanding anything in this section His Majesty may by Order in Council authorize regulations to be made providing for and prescribing the mode of admission of women to the Civil Service of His Majesty and the conditions on which women admitted to that service may be appointed to or continue to hold posts therein and giving power to reserve to men any branch of or posts in the Civil Service in any of His Majesty's possessions overseas or in any foreign country."

When the Bill was in committee, the debate largely centred round this proviso, and Sir Samuel Hoare moved an amendment, the object of which was to make "the conditions of the Civil Service exactly the same for women as for men—with one small exception." It is of interest to find him asserting: "Even before the war I was convinced that no restriction was necessary and that the doors of the Civil Service should be thrown open to women. With the experience of the war I believe that generally is the opinion of almost every honourable member of this House. The Solicitor-General himself paid a well-deserved tribute to the department over which he himself so ably presided during the war in this respect, and his experience has been that of all those who have had direct knowledge of the value of women's work. With that experience in mind it does seem to me to be in every way objectionable to continue this differentiation between the two sexes and leave to Government departments to decide what should be the conditions of the entry of women in the Civil Service. ... The time has come to go over the heads of the bureaucrats in Government offices and insist upon the free admission of women in Government offices on the same conditions as men."

POST-WAR SETTLEMENT AND REORGANIZATION

Undoubtedly there was a great deal of outside support for this view, and probably the member was right who declared, "I think the general public are in favour of women being treated in the same way as men as far as public affairs are concerned and I think this House should realize what the public feeling is." The amendment, however, was lost.

Meanwhile the National Whitley Council for the Administrative and Legal Departments of the Home Civil Service had been set up, and one of its first acts was to appoint a joint committee of staff and official representatives to consider the organization of the clerical classes of the Civil Service. Four women were included on the Committee, one on the official side and three on the staff side. This committee, known as the Reorganization Committee, presented, on February 17th, 1920, an agreed report which was approved by the Government.

Although women had been employed in the service since 1870, the Committee stated that it was not possible "at this stage to attempt a final solution of the novel and complex problems involved in the employment of women side by side with men," and that they were by "common consent breaking new ground." Their endeavour, however, was to ensure that the opportunities afforded to women of proving their fitness to discharge the higher administrative duties of the Civil Service should be full and liberal. They were of the opinion that the existing organization should be considerably simplified. At present the administrative and clerical branches of the service consisted of six classes for men (the first division, the intermediate class, staff clerks, the second division, supervising assistant clerks, and assistant clerks) and six more for women (assistant superintendents, principal clerks, women clerks (first and second classes), shorthand-typists, typists, and writing assistants). The Committee recommended that the following classes should be formed: administrative, executive, clerical, writing assistants, and shorthand-typists and typists—a recommendation which incidentally involved other important changes.

In the first three categories they recommended that women should be given a status and authority identical with that accorded to men; they should be available for employment on the same work and given the widest opportunity of proving their administrative capacity.

In the administrative and executive classes, however, the official side proposed that, for the present, recruitment of women should be by Selection Boards instead of, as in the case of men, an open competition by written examination. The staff side preferred recruitment by written open competitive examination for women as well as for men, but agreed to the Selection Board machinery on the understanding that the method of recruitment should be subject to review in five years.

In regard to the clerical class, the Committee considered that the experimental stage was over (it had been a somewhat long one, just fifty years!). It was an established fact that women were fully capable of discharging the clerical work of the Civil Service, and they recommended that women should be recruited to this class by the same open competition by written examination as the male candidates.

As to the writing assistant class, which had only been in operation in a few departments for large blocks of simple routine work, the Committee recommended that it should continue to be recruited from girls only, but that it should be possible to promote them to the clerical class if found suitable.

The recommendation with regard to shorthand-typists and typists was similar, but it was recognized that men might be employed in this capacity in a few special departmental situations.

The opening of the administrative and executive classes to women was a distinct advance, as was also the institution of a common clerical class for men and women in place of the segregation of women in certain departments.

The Reorganization Report touched on two further points of great importance, the keeping of separate establishment lists for men and women, and the question of segregation *versus* aggregation. These will be more conveniently dealt with later.

On May 19th, 1920, three months after the presentation of the Reorganization Report, a resolution was moved in the House of Commons "that it is expedient that women should have equal opportunity of employment with men in all branches of the Civil Service within the United Kingdom and under all local authorities, and should also receive equal pay." In the debate members were reminded of the manifesto which had been issued before the last election, signed by the Prime Minister and the Lord Privy Seal, which stated that "it was the duty of the Government to remove all existing inequalities of the law as between men and women"; in spite of this manifesto, the proviso to the Sex Disqualification (Removal) Act gave the Government power to regulate the admission of women to the Civil Service and to say who should come in and who

WOMEN SERVANTS OF THE STATE

should not and on what terms. Considerable discussion centred round the recommendation that, whereas men were to be admitted to the administrative grade by open competitive examination, women were to be chosen by a Board of Selection. This system was described as "coming in by the back door" and by what would be represented as patronage. Further, whereas in men's colleges it would be known what the students would have to train for, in order to get into the Civil Service, in women's colleges it would not be known. Who could say what qualities would be demanded by a Board of Selection, which might differ in composition from year to year.

The debate was a lengthy one, but there was practical unanimity in favour of the resolution. Towards the close one of the members congratulated the mover and seconder of the motion on the fact that they had not been able to discover any opponent to it, the only speaker against it being the Financial Secretary to the Treasury. He urged that we must go slowly in altering established custom and rely upon the natural process of evolution. Further, the recommendation in regard to a different entry for women was temporary and the whole subject would come up for revision, but meanwhile those who knew best what administrative work was in the Civil Service felt that there was more chance of the right woman being chosen by a Selection Board than by a written examination.

In the course of the debate the claims of the ex-service men were also discussed, and Major Hills, the mover of the resolution, made it clear that he was entirely in favour of these having first consideration. A clause to this effect was inserted in the resolution and in this form it was agreed to.

POST-WAR SETTLEMENT AND REORGANIZATION

A month later, on June 17th, the Prime Minister was asked whether the Government intended to take action to carry out the resolution. He replied that steps were being taken to give effect to the recommendations of the Reorganization Committee, but that these in the nature of things could only be tentative and that the Government would be prepared to review the situation afresh within a reasonable time, say five years or considerably less.

On July 22nd, 1920, an Order in Council was made in accordance with the terms of the proviso to the Sex Disqualification (Removal) Act. The Government had agreed to give the House of Commons an opportunity of criticizing the detailed regulations made under the Order and accordingly the regulations were laid in draft before Parliament on January 21st, 1921.

These regulations allowed a woman over twenty-two years of age to apply for a post in the administrative class, provided she had served not less than one year in a permanent or temporary clerical or administrative capacity in a Government department or in the war departmental establishments, or as an enrolled member in the Women's Army Auxiliary Corps, the Women's Royal Naval Service, the Women's Royal Air Force Service, or the Voluntary Aid Detachment general service. Candidates judged eligible were required to undergo a simple qualifying examination, and those who passed this examination were to be summoned to an interview before a Selection Board appointed by the Civil Service Commissioners, who would take into account the former record and experience of the candidate.

Similar temporary regulations for the competitive selection of women were drawn up for admission to the executive grade, but with a different age limit, and for a competitive examination governing the appointment of women to posts in the clerical class.

On August 5th, 1921, resolutions were moved in the House of Commons by Major Hills, seconded by Sir Samuel Hoare, requiring that women should be admitted to the service under the same regulations as men, and that women should be appointed to and continue to hold posts in the service under the same regulations, present or future, as governed the classification, remuneration, and other conditions of service of men. Emphasis was laid on the delay which had occurred in dealing with this subject, and the whole ground of equal opportunity and equal pay was again covered, Sir Samuel Hoare asking: "What has happened? The House has declared unanimously for equal treatment of men and women, and yet, when it comes to carrying that into effect, we are faced with Treasury regulations setting up all kinds of checks and balances that are to be applied exclusively to women, making it difficult for women already in the service to be promoted, making vacancies very few for new women to come in and, as my honourable and gallant friend has just said, having the effect of setting up two Civil Services, the one a big and open one for men and the other a restricted and hole-and-corner service for women." Mr. Asquith supported the resolutions. "What you want," he urged, "is to have an efficient Civil Service. Everything must be subordinate to that prime consideration, but you will get an efficient Civil Service, I am satisfied, more easily and in the long run more successfully by throwing open the doors as wide as possible for entrance to examinations and allowing no discrimination purely on account of sex."

The Chancellor of the Exchequer in his reply assured the House that there was "no difference between those who advocate the motion and those who administer the Civil Service as to the object which is to be achieved, namely, that women should have the fullest opportunity of exercising all the functions which in the ordinary way a member of the Civil Service exercises." . . . It was thought that it would be putting women at an unfair disadvantage if they were subjected to the ordinary open competition, and it was believed, and on that belief they acted, that it would give women better opportunities of acquiring the chance of entering the higher grades of the Civil Service if appointments were made "on the basis of selection, at least for a temporary period and until experience showed what women might be able to do in the way of acquiring the necessary knowledge which would enable them to pass these examinations."

He finally moved as an amendment:

"(1) That this House approves of the temporary regulations for competitions governing the appointment of women to situations in the new reorganization classes in the Home Civil Service. Provided that after a provisional period of three years women shall be admitted to the Civil Service of His Majesty within the United Kingdom, under the same regulations, present or future, as provide for and prescribe the mode of admission for men. Provided further that the allocation by the Civil Service Commissioners of such candidates as qualify at the examination shall be made with due regard to the requirements of the situation to be filled.

"(2) That women shall be appointed to and continue to hold posts in the Civil Service within the United Kingdom under the same regulations, present or future, as govern the classification and, in so far as regards status and authority, other conditions of service of men."

The amendment was accepted by Major Hills, subject to the addition of a proviso to safeguard ex-service men, and the resolutions were then passed.

These resolutions brought finality for a time to the discussions in the House of Commons which had been pursued with such vigour, but it was not until 1922, partly owing to the recruitment to the Civil Service being still abnormal, that a special competition was held under the Temporary Regulations, with the result that three appointments of women were made to the administrative class, two to special posts, and thirty-four to posts in the junior executive, higher executive, and higher clerical grades.

The Reorganization Report had recommended drastic changes in the classification for the administrative and clerical branches of the service. These changes necessitated the assimilation of classes, and not only had lines to be laid down for the assimilation of men's classes, but also for the assimilation of men's and women's classes—a somewhat formidable task. The Report had laid down certain general principles to be followed in merging the different classes, and these were gradually put into operation, with the result that the women clerical officers were chiefly drafted into the new clerical class, with the exception of those employed in the writing assistants and typing grades, and comparatively few found themselves in the executive class.

As already mentioned, the Report had touched on two

POST-WAR SETTLEMENT AND REORGANIZATION

further points. The first of these was the question of keeping separate establishment lists for men and women. The Committee recommended that this course should be adopted during the experimental period, and that promotion for men and women should proceed separately as vacancies occurred in the higher establishment reserved for either sex. Thus they were not in favour of a joint seniority list and were in favour of reserved posts. The question, however, was discussed in Parliament, where the placing of men and women on a common seniority list was urged, and as a result a Treasury Committee was set up in 1922, consisting of staff and official representatives of both sexes, to examine and report on the subject, as far as the classes included in the Reorganization Report were concerned. The Committee did not report until March 1924. Its main recommendation was as follows: "Seniority lists are normally used for purposes of leave and promotion. A common measure of seniority as between men and women is therefore required when men and women are employed side by side on similar duties and are considered together for leave and promotion. We recommend that in all departments in which women are employed serious consideration should be given at an early date and in accordance with the recognized departmental procedure to the compilation of common seniority lists."

This report was circulated to departments on April 28th, 1925, under cover of a Treasury circular, in which departments were asked to bring before their departmental Whitley Councils at an early date the question of the compilation of common seniority lists for the classes dealt with in the Reorganization Report. The matter was accordingly put before the Councils concerned, but in many cases the reorganization of the departments had already taken place, leaving the large majority of the women on a separate establishment list, so that little inclination was shown to adopt common seniority lists generally. Gradually, however, some departmental Councils reported in favour of the adoption of the principle, more particularly in regard to grades recruited by competitions open to both sexes.

The second point touched on in the Reorganization Report was one of vital importance to women in its effect on their opportunities and prospects: this was the question of aggregation. In the early days, as has already been recorded, women were segregated; that is to say, they were employed on specialized work in what was termed a woman's branch, with separate seniority lists and avenues of promotion, and were not in direct competition with men. The advantage of this system was that, at any rate in the departmental classes, as for example the inspectorates, women were employed on work for which their experience as women was admitted to be peculiarly valuable. There was a definite *raison d'être* for their employment and it was recognized that on work in connection with women and girls their contribution was essential.

In the non-departmental classes the reason for their employment was in the first instance their cheapness; gradually, however, there emerged other assets in certain characteristics they brought to their work—organizing ability, quickness, and capacity for hard work.

The disadvantages of the system lay in the restriction of the woman's sphere. She was precluded from gaining the experience which would make it possible for her to under-

POST-WAR SETTLEMENT AND REORGANIZATION

take the work in all its aspects and so prove that her special characteristics were of value. Her prospects of promotion were consequently confined within a limited range, and she was kept off the general seniority lists which lead to the highest controlling posts in the service. Her work, although often equal to that of her man colleague, was not identical, and for that reason was often not rated so high. She was not able to show that her particular qualities were of value on all sides of the work.

The war had to a certain extent swept segregation aside. Women had tasted aggregation with its wider scope, more interesting work, and better prospects, and were not inclined to return to their limited field. Departments also had realized what women could do, and some at least were anxious to give them the wider field of work.

The Reorganization Report threw the responsibility of choice as to whether it should be segregation or aggregation on to the departments, with the remark that "it may fairly be argued that in order to obtain the full value of the experiment every opportunity should be given for men and women to work side by side."

Closely allied to the question of aggregation was that of the reservation of posts to men only and to women only.

The Sex Disqualification (Removal) Act had laid down that a woman was not disqualified by sex or marriage from the exercise of any public function. In 1921 the Treasury was advised that this meant "that the woman is not under an inherent disability from holding certain posts because she is a woman or because she is married. In other words the appointment of a woman or a married woman to these posts, if made, would not be invalid. It is quite another thing to say that a woman is *entitled* to be appointed to or to hold any of the specified posts on exactly the same terms as if she were a man, and this in fact is precisely what the Act refrains from saying."

Although there was no formal regulation reserving certain posts to men or women, a considerable number of posts or grades in the Home Civil Service had been designated for men only, or regulations governing admission to the competitions had prescribed that women should not be admitted as candidates. Similarly, there were certain appointments for which it had been decided that women only should be eligible. In some cases, the reason for this differentiation was obvious, in others it was not, and it was difficult to understand how the distinction had arisen.

The proviso to the Act had authorized the making of regulations under Order in Council reserving to men any branch of, or posts in, the Civil Service in any of His Majesty's possessions overseas or in any foreign country. Accordingly under the Order of July 22nd, 1920, regulations were made on August 5th, 1921, excluding women from posts which were in general those overseas. In consequence the practice also grew up of reserving for men posts in the administrative work in home departments which dealt with overseas affairs.

Thus, during the years immediately succeeding the war, departments were faced, for their consideration, with a number of principles governing the future employment of women.

In 1929 a Royal Commission on the Civil Service, appointed under the chairmanship of Lord Tomlin, pronounced that, speaking generally, the best course to follow

POST-WAR SETTLEMENT AND REORGANIZATION

was the policy of "a fair field and no favour," which carried with it the adoption of aggregation, and that, so far as possible, all posts in the service should be open to men and women, "subject to modification in regard to those areas of the service in which the reservation of certain posts to men or women is demanded in the public interest or where it is necessary to employ a certain minimum proportion of men or of women in each grade." They held that, until men and women had had opportunities of working side by side, no one could forecast, in regard to many occupations, whether a man or woman would prove most suited for them, and that the existence of prejudice was not sufficient justification for excluding women from posts, "since the prejudice, if it exists, can only be combated by giving women an opportunity of overcoming it." It is of considerable interest that this Commission openly recognized the prejudice which women have had for so many years to combat and which they have so successfully overcome.

In regard to the reservation of posts, they said this was not a question which was capable of determination once and for all; but in existing circumstances they considered that certain categories of posts, which they enumerated, should continue to be reserved for men.

From 1929 the words "fair field and no favour" became a part of the Civil Service vocabulary, but they were not new. Fifty years earlier, Mr. Cooke Taylor, in a paper before the Social Science Congress at Manchester, had begged the State to give women a fair field and not to extend its favour, a very strong line to take in those days.

In 1934 various matters in regard to the position of women arising out of this Report were submitted for consideration to a committee of the National Whitley Council known as the Committee on Women's Questions. It was agreed by them to recommend departments to undertake, through appropriate machinery for joint discussion, an immediate review of reservations operating within the department, and publicly to state the reason for these reservations, and that, within a period not exceeding three years, there should be a general review of the situation by a joint central body. In regard to aggregation the Committee agreed with the Royal Commission's view, and recommended that a departmental examination of the ways and means of placing staffing arrangements on an aggregated basis should forthwith be instituted, and that there should be a general review of the subject by a joint central body at the end of a period not exceeding five years.

These, then, were the general principles affecting the employment of women civil servants, which were under discussion in the post-war years. The changes which had taken place and were taking place were far-reaching and progressive and would, indeed, have astonished even Mr. Scudamore. How far these principles were adopted in the different departments and in the various classes of the service is the next subject for review.

CHAPTER 4

WOMEN IN THE TREASURY CLASSES

THE Reorganization Committee in 1919 recognized that it had "become more than ever an imperative necessity so to reconstruct the Civil Service as to enable it to discharge with increasing efficiency its primary functions of advising and assisting Ministers of the Crown; of implementing the policy prescribed by Ministers and by Parliament; and of carrying on the day-to-day administration of the King's Government." In order that these functions might be properly carried out, the Committee, as we have seen, recommended the formation of five Treasury classes, a recommendation which was adopted by the Government in 1920. The first four of these, the administrative, the executive, the clerical and the writing assistant classes, were to be common to the service although not necessarily to be found in all departments, and were to deal with work of an "administrative-clerical sphere."

THE ADMINISTRATIVE CLASS

The duties which the Reorganization Committee considered would be appropriate to the administrative class were concerned "with the formation of policy, with the co-ordination and improvement of Government machinery and with the general administration and control of the departments of the public service." For the performance of these duties it was evident that officers with the highest standard of educational qualifications were needed. In order to ensure that such should be appointed, the Committee recommended the recruitment of men officers between twenty-two and twenty-four years of age by means of an open competitive examination in the subjects embraced by the various honours courses of the universities. This class should also "be open to all men and women already employed in the service who show early proof of real ability and promise of being able to discharge, in the course of time, higher administrative functions." The men and women so recruited should be regarded as a cadet corps from which selection should be made to higher administrative posts, and the administrative staff should comprise assistant principals, principals, assistant secretaries, principal assistant secretaries, and finally heads of departments and their deputies.

From the Armistice to the end of 1924, recruitment to the Civil Service was quite abnormal. War-time staffs had to be reduced and the ex-service man provided for, and the process of assimilation had to operate. It was therefore found necessary to suspend the normal open competitions for the administrative class between the years 1921 and 1925.

Meanwhile, as has been said, a special competition for women had been held and three appointments of women made to the administrative class, one woman being allocated to the Ministry of Pensions and the others to the Treasury and the Board of Education, the departments in which they had been previously employed, and two women were appointed to special posts. In addition, a few women who were already established found their way into the administrative class as assistant principals and principals, and two others became assistant secretaries, Miss Durham, in the Ministry of Labour, a post she held until her retirement,

WOMEN IN THE TREASURY CLASSES

and, in 1929, Miss Ritson, in the Department of Health for Scotland, who became Assistant Secretary and Controller of Insurance and Pensions.

In 1925 the open competition for the administrative class was resumed, and now for the first time women competed on equal terms with men for these high posts in the service. The result at first was encouraging. Eighty men and twenty-seven women sat for the examination and nineteen men and three women were appointed, the women taking up duty as assistant principals in the Ministry of Health, Board of Trade and Public Record Office.

In 1926, however, only twelve women sat for the examination and one was appointed. From that time the number of women sitting for the examination was disappointing—in 1927 to 1935 (nine years) only eighty-eight women competed, of whom eight were successful.

By 1934 it had become evident that there must be some deterrents operating to prevent women from becoming candidates. Enquiries showed that women usually finished their university career at the age of twenty-one and were then generally obliged for financial reasons either to get work at once or begin their training for teaching, where they could be fairly certain of obtaining a post. They felt that the chance of getting a position in the administrative class was too remote to justify them in postponing this training for at least a year; also they often had not funds available for coaching, which was considered advisable by the majority of candidates as a preparation for this examination, the difficulty of which had often become exaggerated in their minds and had been allowed to overshadow the interesting and important work which a post of this kind brought with it. Further, it became apparent that in some colleges women were not being encouraged to take this examination or indeed having their attention drawn to it. Gradually the matter was given publicity, addresses were delivered to the students at the women's colleges, Appointment Boards became busy and loan funds began giving advances to suitable candidates for special coaching. The results surpassed expectation. In 1936 seventeen women competed and six were successful, while in the following year twenty-nine competed and eight were successful. *The Times* of January 31st, 1938, drew special attention to the women's successes in the examination. It was pointed out that university women were now showing a preference for subjects hitherto regarded as a field for men. "Political organization was one of the optional subjects chosen by one woman, in which she scored 75 per cent. Another plumped for general economics, industry and trade, public finance, economic history, and English literature, her respective scores being 78, 79, 69, 76, and 90 per cent. Two competitors chose the same subjects, namely metaphysics, moral philosophy, logic, and psychology. They proved that logic is no longer a male characteristic, for in this subject they were awarded respectively 74 and 88 per cent. Of more than 400 in the examination no man reached this level."

The Gladstone Committee stated in 1919 that the evidence they had taken convinced them that, "having regard to the existing differences in the opportunities of education and in the general mental equipment of young men and women, it would be unsafe to introduce women forthwith as interchangeable with men, throughout the various departments, and that a readjustment of this kind needed to be worked

WOMEN IN THE TREASURY CLASSES

out by gradual processes and carefully tested stage by stage." The opportunities of education and the general mental equipment of young university women are evidently now not so different from that of the young university man. Indeed, at the administrative class examinations in 1937, on the written test alone, two of the women would have taken first and second places and another woman the fourth place; they lost, however, on the interview. Undoubtedly this examination need not now hold any terrors for the good university woman candidate.

Women have found an entry into the administrative class in all the main departments, with the exception of the three Defence Departments, where the practice has arisen of reserving the administrative posts for men. Whether this practice is a wise one, with war clouds always hanging over us, is a question which the future will decide.

In any case, women are now employed equally with men in a class of the service where the highest work is carried on, and the fact that a number have already been promoted to the principal grade and one to the assistant secretary grade shows that they are able to carry out the duties of these posts.

THE EXECUTIVE CLASS

To the executive class the Reorganization Committee assigned the higher work of supply and accounting departments and of other executive or specialized branches of the Civil Service. In the junior ranks the work includes "critical examination of particular cases of lesser importance not clearly within the scope of approved regulations or general decisions, initial investigations into matters of higher importance; ... while in the upper ranges it is concerned with the settlement of broad questions arising out of business in hand or in contemplation and with the responsible conduct of important operations." It is obvious that the work in this class covers a wide and important field, and that officers with a good education, initiative, resource, and a sound judgment have great opportunities before them.

The Committee recommended that the recruitment to this class should be by open competitive written examination between the ages of eighteen and nineteen, and also by promotion from the clerical class, and that women employed in it should be given a status and authority identical with that accorded to men.

At first this class was formed by the assimilation of pre-reorganization classes, and a few women found their way into it by this means. The special competition for women held in 1922 also resulted in the appointment of a few more qualified women. There was however a redundancy of men in this class owing to assimilation, and accordingly no open competition could be held until 1928. When it was held, 285 boys and 315 girls entered for the examination, and of the 135 candidates declared successful 52 were girls. By 1930, however, there were 440 boys and 326 girls, and from that time the number of boys sitting steadily increased, the girls remaining more or less stationary.

Still, in view of the far larger proportion of boy candidates, the number of successful girls has been reasonably high. The positions filled from this examination include, not only those in the executive class, but also those of assistant, examiners in the Inland Revenue Estate Duty Department, assistant auditors in the Exchequer and Audit Department,

WOMEN IN THE TREASURY CLASSES

and audit assistants in the Ministry of Health District Audit Staff; also assistant inspectors in the Ministry of Health Insurance Department and actuarial assistants in the Government Actuary's Department. Thus by this examination many new opportunities for interesting work with good prospects have been thrown open to women and are being filled by them. The posts in the executive class in the Defence Departments alone are reserved to men, on account of women's inability for service overseas.

CLERICAL CLASSES

The Reorganization Committee entrusted to this class all the simple clerical duties in public departments in so far as these were not assigned to writing assistants, and they enunciated the opinion, without a shadow of doubt, that women were fully capable of discharging the clerical work of the Civil Service. The pre-war women clerks had made this quite clear; indeed, the Gladstone Committee paid a high tribute to the ability and value of the permanent women clerks employed in the Post Office, Ministry of Labour, and Board of Education, and were satisfied that great advantage would have been derived if they had been utilized as trainers and supervisors of women clerks in war departments.

The clerical class was built up by means of assimilation of pre-reorganization classes and by means of examinations of candidates with service in a temporary clerical capacity. As a result of such examinations held from 1919 onwards, 2,920 women obtained appointments in the general and departmental classes. The Reorganization Committee also recommended that there should be direct recruitment to the clerical class by open competitive written examination. It was

WOMEN SERVANTS OF THE STATE

not found possible, however, to hold such an examination for boys and girls until November 1927, although special competitions open to girls only were held in 1922, 1925, and May 1927, to fill vacancies for clerical posts in women's branches.

From 1927 boys and girls have competed equally for appointments and there has been a steady flow of girls finding their way into this class, where interesting work under good conditions is open to them. A number have obtained promotion, so that women are now employed in all grades of the clerical classes, including the most senior. In the administrative, executive, and clerical grades of the Treasury class there is no segregation, women and men are employed on the same work and have the same opportunities and are more or less on a common seniority list. It has been proved beyond question that the fears expressed in regard to the capacity of women to perform work in the administrative-clerical sphere were groundless.

WRITING ASSISTANTS AND SHORTHAND-TYPISTS

The work of women in the Treasury classes would be incomplete without reference to their employment in the writing assistant (now called clerical assistant) class and the shorthand-typist and typist class—classes which under the Reorganization Report have been confined to women.

The writing assistant class was established in 1915 in the Post Office and spread into a few other departments, the work consisting of routine and some clerical duties. The Reorganization Committee recommended that the employment of writing assistants should be extended wherever there were large blocks of simple routine work of a similar character to be performed, although they did not intend this class to be treated as one common to the whole service.

After the war temporary women clerks were given the opportunity of entering this class by special examination and about 3,400 were appointed. The Committee recommended that the class should be recruited by local competitive examinations of a simple character, with age limits of sixteen and seventeen, and this has been done, with the result that there are to-day about 10,500 clerical assistants in the service. This examination has attracted a good type of girl candidate, and every year it has been found possible to promote a fair number to the clerical grade.

The Tomlin Commission gave special consideration to this class and came to the conclusion that for one reason it was well for it to be confined to girls. A turnover of staff on work of this routine character is advisable, and the retirement of women on marriage is therefore an important factor.

The shorthand-typist and typist classes have grown beyond all expectation, and, whereas in 1914 about 600 women were employed on these duties, to-day there are about 10,000, including supervisory posts.

It is not "only important letters, such as those to the Treasury," which are typed, but every kind of letter, and to every class of correspondent, even the humblest. "My Lords of the Treasury" were indeed out in their calculations when they said in 1894 that it was not probable that the class of women typists in the service would be very numerous. The Civil Service to-day without the typist class is impossible to visualize, and no one would deny that it would be impossible to carry on without the help of these women servants of the State.

SPECIAL POSTS FOR WOMEN

With the extension of the employment of women in the service, it was thought in some quarters that a woman should be appointed on the establishment divisions of departments to advise on and deal with questions arising in connection with their employment. During the war period, when staffs were rapidly recruited, the practice had arisen of appointing a woman with duties of this nature, and hence it was thought that some such post would continue to be necessary. Accordingly, women were appointed as Director of Women Establishments (the first holder of this post being the Hon. Dame Maude Lawrence) Women Establishment Officers, Principal Lady Superintendents, Controllers of Women's Staff, Superintendents of Female Staff, and so forth, their duties being confined to women. Two of the women recruited by the special competition in 1923 were assigned to posts of this kind, and others were promoted to them.

In practice, however, after a transitional period had elapsed, these posts were not found to be altogether satisfactory. Men's and women's establishment problems are not so different in nature as to require separate treatment and are more justly dealt with when considered as one question. Moreover, a post, which under segregation might carry with it specific duties, did not necessarily do so under aggregation; when chiefly advisory, with no certainty that the advice proffered would be acted upon, it was not altogether satisfactory to the holder, whilst it gave a false feeling of

WOMEN IN THE TREASURY CLASSES

security to the women. The woman holding such a post, if assiduous in her duties, was inclined to be a source of irritation, and if inactive became a laughing-stock, while she herself was only gaining one-sided and limited experience instead of performing all the duties of the grade, which would qualify her for promotion to higher posts. Further, it was found that, as Whitley organization developed in the service, it was wiser to allow "women's questions" to be handled on a broader basis by means of Whitley Committees, on which women could, and indeed should, serve.

Gradually, therefore, these special posts for women in connection with establishment questions have been discontinued, and any of the functions belonging to them which were of special use have been transferred to women who are employed on establishment and engaged on work common to men and women. The fact has not been overlooked in many departments that it is advisable to employ women in grades high enough to secure their representation on Whitley Councils, since it is recognized that the addition of some women to a team adds to its general range of experience and capacity.

CHAPTER 5

WOMEN IN THE DEPARTMENTS

BROADLY speaking, the Treasury classes are the classes doing administrative-clerical work which is common to the service. In addition, however, there are officers engaged on clerical work peculiar to individual departments; amongst these a large number are women. There are also departmental classes engaged on various other duties, many of which are of a specialist nature, and women are employed in these also.

It is impossible to give a complete survey of the employment of women in all the departments. It is proposed therefore first to sketch shortly the present position of women's employment in the departments mentioned in Chapter 1, and then deal with those which have more recently introduced women into their ranks.

THE POST OFFICE

It had not required a world war to establish the fact that the employment of women in the Post Office was essential to the nation, and in the readjustment which took place in post-war days there was no going back on the experiment which had been tried with fear and trembling in 1870 and which had proved so successful.

Indeed, by 1929, in the Accountant-General's Department the number of men and women was approximately equal, in the Savings Bank Department women considerably outnumbered the men, while the Money Order Department

WOMEN IN THE DEPARTMENTS

was largely a women's department. In the accounting section of the more recently established office, the London Telephone Service, women were in the majority. In all these departments they were employed on executive and clerical work of all kinds.

On the other hand, in the headquarters departments, in the Engineering and Store departments and in the offices of the Controllers of the London Postal Service and of the Central Telegraph Office the clerical work was done chiefly by men.

On the manipulative side, practically the whole of the telephone operating between 8 a.m. and 8 p.m. was in the hands of women, and they were largely employed on telegraph and counter duties. Indeed, there were about 20,000 women telephonists and 8,000 women employed as telegraphists and at the public counters, for which class of work they were considered to be especially suitable.

Although the employment of women had increased to such a remarkable extent, they were, except in the London Telephone Service, in the main employed in separate branches on different sections of the work; hence they were segregated. Further, they had separate seniority lists with separate avenues for promotion, the hierarchy on the women's side running up to a Lady Superintendent and on the men's side to the Controller.

Although in some sections the work assigned to men and women was practically the same—as regards the clerical work of the London Telephone Service it was identical—broadly speaking, so the Secretary to the Post Office, Sir Evelyn Murray, told the Tomlin Commission, the superior work was given to the men and the more routine work to the women. This system, he said, was largely historical, as was also the system of separate seniority lists, "a system of organization which had been handed down and which it has been in nobody's interest to change."

The net effect of this segregation was that the avenues of promotion for women were more limited than was the case for men. The Tomlin Commission in their Report recognized that the main question in regard to women's employment in the Post Office was whether this system should be continued. They recommended that the accepted policy in the clerical classes should be aggregation, but that the change should be effected gradually. They pointed out that "as and when aggregation is introduced many higher supervisory posts at present reserved to men will *ipso facto* be opened to both sexes." In regard to the manipulative staffs they doubted whether it was possible to introduce aggregation.

In accordance with present-day practice this question, with its important implications, has been considered by the Post Office departmental Whitley Council, and gradually aggregation and common seniority lists are being introduced. The women have no longer as their goal a Lady Superintendentship, but the Controllership, women now taking their place with men in the higher controlling posts. Instead of being employed on duties which might be regarded as of an inferior kind, they are slowly taking their share of all the clerical work, a change which will of course only reach completion in course of time.

In view of the fact that the very first women civil servants were telegraph operators, it is interesting to note that many have now risen to positions where technical knowledge is required and for this purpose have taken and passed technical

WOMEN IN THE DEPARTMENTS

and departmental examinations and have acquired a knowledge of the mechanical and electrical parts of the telegraph apparatus. Indeed a few women are now participating with men in technical and maintenance work.

MINISTRY OF HEALTH

The Ministry of Health was formed under the Ministry of Health Act 1919, and to it were transferred amongst other matters all the powers and duties of the Local Government Board and of the National Health Insurance Commission and those of the Board of Education with respect to the medical inspection and treatment of children.

Thus from the first women were employed in this Ministry. By 1930, of the total staff of 6,237 persons, 2,316 were women and of the 486 employed in the Welsh Board of Health, 170 were women.

The Local Government Board had no women's branches and was staffed almost entirely by men, except for the few women inspectors who assisted them and inspected Poor Law infirmaries and the work of committees concerned with the boarding-out of Poor Law children. These women were taken over by the Ministry of Health, and in 1920 the post formerly held by Miss Stansfield was resuscitated, Miss Wamsley, who had been appointed in 1913, being made Superintendent Inspector.

In February 1919 Sir George Newman, Chief Medical Inspector of the Board of Education and also of the Local Government Board, was transferred with his staff to the Ministry of Health. From that date women doctors were employed in this Ministry, but they were confined to the work of maternity and child welfare and were not regarded as interchangeable with their men colleagues until 1936, when the system of reserving posts was given up. A few women inspectors (trained nurses with the C.M.B. certificate) were appointed in 1919 to assist the women medical officers.

In 1925 it was decided to amalgamate the two staffs of women inspectors and place them under the woman Senior Medical Officer as regards general supervision, and Miss Wamsley was made an Assistant General Inspector, with duties of the same type as those of the men holding this rank. This post she held until her retirement in 1931, after which it was not filled by a woman. There is no man's grade corresponding to this grade of woman inspector, which at present numbers seven women, and they have no avenue of promotion.

Matters relating to the welfare and training of the blind have also been entrusted to this department, and for this purpose three inspectors, one of whom is a woman, are employed.

The National Health Insurance Commission employed by 1919 a large number of women inspectors, working on segregated lines and with their sphere of action restricted to certain trades in which woman's labour largely predominated. In 1927, after an exhaustive review of the position, it was decided that the nature of the work generally did not render it necessary or desirable that the staff should be segregated and that women were competent to undertake the full scope of the duties equally with their male colleagues. Accordingly, in November 1928, aggregation of work came into being and the previous restrictions on women's work disappeared. Sir Arthur Robinson, Permanent Secretary to the Ministry of Health, later informed the Tomlin Commission that the relative efficiency of men and women as inspectors was "just about the same."

The Report of the Royal Commission on the care and control of the Feeble-Minded (published in 1908) recommended the appointment of at least one woman as a commissioner on the reconstituted central authority. The Lord Chancellor, presumably recognizing the desirability of this recommendation, decided that he would not wait for the legislation necessary to reconstitute the Lunacy Commission and that he would, under the relevant sections of the Lunacy Act of 1890, appoint a woman as an unpaid commissioner. Accordingly in 1908 he offered the position to a woman who was known to have had the experience which would qualify her for appointment. His offer was accepted, but after the lapse of a few days it was represented to him that he could not make the appointment as he had no power to appoint a woman, and he was therefore obliged to withdraw his offer. It was not until the Mental Deficiency Act was passed in 1913 that women were made eligible for commissionerships both paid and unpaid.

The Board of Control, for which the Minister of Health is responsible to Parliament, was established under this Act, and to it were transferred all the powers and duties of the Commissioners in Lunacy under the Lunacy Acts 1890–1911, the Commissioners becoming members of the Board. The same woman who had previously been offered a commissionership in Lunacy was appointed as a commissioner on the new Board. At the present time the Board consists of five senior commissioners, including one woman, and twelve commissioners, of whom three are women, two with medical and one with legal qualifications. In addition, there are four women inspectors to assist with the visitation of the mental patients.

In this Ministry women are to be found in practically all the grades, including not only the Treasury classes, but also the District Audit staff and that of the Accountant-General's Department. Generally speaking, it has been the policy of the Ministry to employ men and women on the same work and to regard them as interchangeable. The tendency has been to ensure that both should have equal opportunities of showing their respective merits on the work of the various sections of the department, and supervising officers of both sexes in control of mixed staffs of men and women have gradually become the order of the day. The question of common seniority lists has been under consideration by the departmental Whitley Council. The practice has been that, when vacancies occur in the higher grades, they are normally filled by the promotion of men or women according to the sex of the previous holder of the post; when new posts are created, both men and women are considered together.

BOARD OF EDUCATION

The woman inspectorate which Sir Robert Morant had established continued to develop, but little change was made in its organization. The senior posts, which were of a specialist nature, were increased and converted into staff posts, and the divisional women staff inspectors, as they were now called, were allocated, one to Wales and one to each of the nine territorial divisions for general work in all branches, acting under the divisional inspector.

WOMEN IN THE DEPARTMENTS

Two of these women continued to act as responsible advisers to the Board on domestic subjects and on technical education for women and girls throughout the country.

The position of the woman staff inspector of training colleges remained specialized as before, but with increased status and responsibility.

The women inspectors, however, continued to form a separate corps under the Chief Woman Inspector. "Generally speaking," so the Tomlin Commission was informed, "their primary function is to secure that, as far as possible, the woman's aspect of education in every grade and the needs of girls and women in all kinds of education are adequately realized and borne in mind in the work of the department both in the inspectorate and the office."

They did not, however, undertake the charge of districts or divisions, but acted as advisers and assistants to the district and divisional inspectors. Although they were all H.M. Inspectors, their sphere of responsibility was in the main distinct from that of their men colleagues.

In 1930 the whole question of the inspectorate of the Board of Education came before the Tomlin Commission for consideration, the Inspectors' Association, which included the women inspectors, submitting statements and giving evidence. At that time there were sixty-three women inspectors working in elementary, secondary, and technical schools and in training colleges and doing specialized work in domestic subjects and physical training, the work differing widely in character, with varying degrees of responsibility.

Generally speaking, in the elementary school branch, the quality and quantity of the work assigned to the woman was not officially defined and was left to be determined by the man under whom she worked. The arrangements made by the men district inspectors showed extreme variation. In some districts the woman was given considerable scope and authority, in others the reverse was the case.

The woman inspector of the secondary schools enjoyed a larger measure of responsibility, but here again her scope was limited, for the men inspectors were in administrative charge of the districts and were the Board's spokesmen with the officials of the local education authority in all general matters of policy.

There were also seven women inspectors who, in addition to other duties, were specially concerned with the instruction provided for women and girls in technical and evening schools. These women had direct access to the local education authority but were expected to keep the district inspector informed of matters discussed. The inspectors of domestic subjects had also direct access to the local education authorities.

Finally, the training colleges for women teachers were assigned to women inspectors, and for the inspection and administrative duties in connection with these they had complete responsibility. This position had been held since 1910 and marked the recognition by Sir Robert Morant of the claim of women to hold posts of responsibility equally with men.

Sir Aubrey Symonds, when giving evidence before the Commission, stated that women were introduced into the inspectorate exclusively for the purpose of assisting the male inspectors, and the Board, in the performance of certain special functions in regard to which it was desirable to have

WOMEN IN THE DEPARTMENTS

the assistance of women. Further, that the practice in regard to the inspectorate conformed with the policy pronounced in 1904.

The disadvantages of the existing position were enumerated in the following statement which the women inspectors submitted to the Commission:

"The women inspectors have never been incorporated into the main organization of the inspectorate.

"Such responsibility as the women enjoy is, as a general rule, delegated responsibility. The divisional and district inspectorships are held by men only.

"The work allocated to women inspectors in the different branches varies greatly in scope and responsibility, notwithstanding that they are all in the same grade.

"In the elementary branch the work of the woman inspector is officially undefined, and is therefore mainly dependent upon the individual arrangements made by the district inspector, a situation which leaves the woman inspector in an invidious and uncertain position detrimental alike to contentment and efficiency.

"It is customary in the Board to restrict the work of women inspectors to matters dealing with their own sex and with younger children, whereas in the interests of education as a whole, there should, in the opinion of women inspectors, be full co-operation between men and women inspectors."

They stressed two further points of great importance: "Women have never been selected for any of the chief positions on the intellectual side of the work. The staff inspectorships for subjects, e.g. English, music, mathematics, are assigned to men only, and the chief examinerships of subjects, except in the case of needlework and domestic subjects and physical training, have never been assigned to women.

"Women inspectors are not, as a matter of course, called to conferences on educational and administrative policy to which their men colleagues are called, nor are they adequately represented on standing committees, or on committees set up for special purposes. It is obvious that women inspectors cannot make their full contribution to the work of the Board unless they take part in the deliberations relating to educational problems which arise."

One of the recommendations made by the women inspectors was that all grades, positions, and types of work in the present or any future organization of the inspectorate should be open equally to men and women. In this contention they had the support of some of their men colleagues. Mr. Hankin, for instance, declared before the Commission: "My feeling is that most of the work of an inspector can be done equally well by a man or a woman; there are certain cases in which a woman is necessary, just as in certain cases a man is necessary. The vast bulk of the work, it seems to me, can be carried out by either a man or a woman. I suppose that, in certain parts of the educational world, you still find some prejudice against women, but I think that prejudice is disappearing. I think that we shall see a gradual process of women taking their natural position in the educational service without much worrying whether the work is done by a man or a woman."

The Commission after careful consideration recommended that the accepted policy of the Board in regard to their inspectorate should be complete aggregation, but that this could only be reached by stages.

WOMEN IN THE DEPARTMENTS

This recommendation has been and is being put into operation, and one woman was appointed as divisional inspector and others as district inspectors, with all the responsibilities and authority which these posts carry.

In 1908 a Medical Department was established in the Board, charged with the supervision of matters relating to the health of school-children. The responsibility for their medical inspection and treatment was transferred from the Board to the Ministry of Health in 1919, but arrangements were made for the Board to continue the central administration of this service as agents for the Ministry. Forming part of the department, under a senior medical officer, is a staff of six medical officers, of whom two are women, and these act as expert advisers and undertake the necessary inspection of the local authorities' school medical service, special schools, etc. There are also a staff inspector and nine inspectors of physical training, of whom seven are women. A senior medical officer of the Ministry of Health acts by arrangement as Chief Woman Medical Adviser to the Board.

MINISTRY OF LABOUR

The Ministry of Labour was created by the New Ministries and Secretaries Act, 1916, which provided for the transfer to it of certain powers and duties of the Board of Trade in relation to trade and industry. The transfer became effective on January 10th, 1917, and from that date the principal functions of the Ministry consisted of the maintenance of the national system of employment exchanges, the administration of the national scheme of unemployment insurance, the dealing with questions affecting the relations between employers and employed, the administration of the Trade

Boards Act, the publication of information relating to labour conditions, and, later, the transaction of the British Government business connected with the International Labour Organization.

Women had already been engaged, in pre-war days as well as during the war, on duties connected with certain of these functions, so they naturally came to be employed in this new department from its inception. Indeed, the creation of this Ministry meant little more in some quarters than a change of title. On April 1st, 1930, they numbered rather more than one-quarter of the total staff, there being 4,885 women among the total staff of 17,104, and they were to be found in all grades.

Much of the work in this Ministry entails human contacts and provides an interesting sphere for women desiring to serve the State.

Following the recommendation of the Reorganization Report a committee of the departmental Whitley Council was set up in February 1921 to consider the general principles of segregation or aggregation, and an analysis of the work performed by the Ministry was made under the following heads: (*a*) necessarily women's work; (*b*) more appropriately women's work; (*c*) work common to both sexes; (*d*) more appropriately men's work; (*e*) necessarily men's work.

It was agreed that in the employment exchanges the work of dealing with the general public in the men's departments of the exchanges should be classified as necessarily men's work, the corresponding duties in the women's departments as necessarily women's work, and the managing of mixed exchanges and general inspection of mixed exchanges as more appropriately men's work.

WOMEN IN THE DEPARTMENTS

The assignment of the work as between men and women proceeded broadly on the above basis, although, as the years passed, more of the work came to be regarded as common to both sexes. A woman was appointed a Deputy Divisional Controller, and her new duties required her to devote much of her time to matters connected with the men's departments of the exchanges. Then a woman was appointed manager of a mixed exchange, and another was given charge of the men's side of an exchange, while women shared equally with their men colleagues the work in the divisional offices.

In regard to inspection under the Trade Boards Act, as has already been pointed out, women had from the first equal opportunities with their men colleagues, so under the analysis this form of inspection was naturally regarded as common to both sexes. In view, however, of the large numbers of women employed in the trades concerned, it was recognized that a substantial proportion of the posts should be held by women. Thus employers from the first became accustomed to dealing with women in regard to the wages they paid their workers, and the Permanent Secretary of the Ministry of Labour, when asked by the Tomlin Commission whether women inspectors of the Trade Board were hampered by prejudice in their contact with trade unions and employers, was able to reply, "fortunately there we were able to fall in line with the Home Office tradition and the general inspectorate tradition, which seems to have included women inspectors." Undoubtedly, if prejudice can be overcome in the duties of inspection, fears that it may hamper women's work generally are groundless.

WOMEN SERVANTS OF THE STATE

The same witness informed the Commission that women were regarded as eligible for promotion to all grades, and that opportunities of advancement on their merits to higher posts had been afforded to them; in his department women had the same status as the men and they had "some very good work done by the women officers in all grades."

As a result of the report of the Committee on Women's Questions, the whole question of segregation and aggregation was reviewed again in 1937 and the existing practice in the main confirmed. To-day there are seven women in charge of mixed exchanges in different parts of the country, while several are the recognized deputy managers of such exchanges.

The Minister of Labour is also responsible to Parliament since 1934 for a new and important department, the Unemployment Assistance Board.

THE UNEMPLOYMENT ASSISTANCE BOARD

This Board was charged by the Unemployment Assistance Act of 1934 "with the duty of creating a new social service for the assistance of able-bodied unemployed persons who normally are wage-earners, not only for the relief of their material needs but also for the promotion of their welfare." Here indeed was an interesting field for women's work and one after their own heart. Women have formed by now a fine tradition of social service in many different spheres, and in the work of the Unemployment Assistance Board there was an opportunity of social work of a high order and of a professional character which had a great appeal.

From its inception women were considered equally with men for the numerous posts under the Board, aggregation

WOMEN IN THE DEPARTMENTS

being introduced from the first. Women were chosen, although not in great numbers, for positions in nearly all the grades, with the same titles and the same duties as their men colleagues.

The district officers, men and women, have great responsibilities and large staffs to control, and it is of interest to find women in charge of districts where the staff consists of approximately 200 men and 20 women.

The reports of these officers, which are published in the annual report of the Unemployment Assistance Board, are full of human interest. They also show that women officials are well able to co-operate in a friendly way with local authorities and voluntary organizations, as well as to take their share in general administration and work in connection with Appeal Tribunals.

HOME OFFICE

Perhaps the greatest development in the use made of the services of women has taken place in the Factory Department of the Home Office. As has been already recorded, the woman inspectorate in the early days was built on a sound and sure foundation, and the women had been encouraged. It was largely due to Sir Malcolm Delevingne, Deputy Under-Secretary of State, who from the very early days was quite unprejudiced and believed in making use of their services, that the women inspectors had been given a great opportunity. They were from the first granted equal powers with their men colleagues as far as women's trades were concerned; they formed their own standard of inspection, and it was a high one. They established contact with the workers by doing what the Chief Inspector of 1879 con-

WOMEN SERVANTS OF THE STATE

sidered unnecessary, questioning the "females." They visited them at home, made meticulous inspections of the factory, and prosecuted whenever necessary. Although in some quarters their methods may not have been appreciated, the best employers welcomed their services.

During the war their duties were extended and they gained more knowledge and experience in technical questions. As the men inspectors were allowed to join the colours or were transferred to other departments, the women took over their work and thus gained an entry to those factories which had hitherto been inspected only by men. At the close of the war the day of judgment came.

On August 5th, 1921, Mr. Asquith said in the House: "I have always acknowledged and have done my best to give effect to the view that as regards the great professions and particularly the services of the State women ought to be placed on precise equality with men. . . . When I was at the Home Office nearly thirty years ago I introduced the appointment for the first time of women as inspectors of factories. It was considered by the State officials at that date to be a terrible proposition, they shook their heads and they did not sleep comfortably at nights. . . . It was suggested that the women would get their petticoats in the machines and there would be loss of life, and also it was suggested that it would be most unseemly that they should go about at night alone in the workshops. . . . We have advanced. We made a very modest beginning in the admission of women to the inspectorate in those days and we have not gone back on it in any way. On the contrary it has been developed upon an ever-increasing scale and all must admit . . . that it has had most beneficial results. . . .

WOMEN IN THE DEPARTMENTS

I only give it by way of illustration to show how efficient women, when they *are* put to it, can discharge functions in the service of the State which up to a very short time ago were jealously reserved for our own sex."

But it was not only in the House of Commons that the work of women was weighed up. A departmental committee was appointed, under the chairmanship of Sir Malcolm Delevingne, to consider amongst other matters the organization of the factory inspectorate, with special reference to the measures necessary for co-ordinating the work of men and women inspectors in the event of the number of women inspectors being increased. As has already been recorded, the women inspectors were at first peripatetic and inspected wherever their services were needed. This led to overlapping and some difficulties in organization as their number increased. In 1908, therefore, the women were assigned to divisions and became to a certain extent a part of the divisional organization, often working in the same offices as their men colleagues, but still under their own woman head. In this way the value of their work came to be more recognized by the men inspectors, and in 1920 the Chief Inspector, Sir Malcolm Robinson, was strongly in favour of giving the women still more responsibility, with the definite status of District Inspector and Superintending Inspector.

The committee heard evidence from all sides and as a result recommended an important scheme of reorganization of the Factory Department.

The following were some of the chief features of the scheme. The men's and women's sides of the inspectorate were amalgamated into a single organization, the posts formerly held by women being abolished, and women inspectors were regarded as eligible for *all* posts. A woman became a deputy chief inspector, two others became superintending inspectors and eight became district inspectors.

The duties of all these women inspectors, as well as of the junior women, were identical with those of the men inspectors, and women were now put in charge of districts and of divisions as superintending inspectors with staffs consisting chiefly of men, and became responsible also for men's trades with their special problems.

A few women inspectors, with the title of Woman Deputy Superintending Inspector, were still retained for special duties in regard to women's work, working in divisions under men superintending inspectors, and there were certain matters chiefly relating to men's employment which were left to the men inspectors; but, broadly speaking, from now on the bulk of the work of inspection was regarded as common to both men and women, and the services of the latter were used for the protection of the men in industry as well as the women. "Let the women inspectors come into our shops," said a bold man trade unionist, and they went. In fact there was an almost complete amalgamation of duties, though separate establishments of men and women were maintained.

Needless to say, it was a great change for all concerned and one which was met with some misgiving in certain quarters, and tact and understanding were needed on the part of the inspectorate if it was to be a success. Generally speaking the inspectorate responded and both men and women did their best to make the new organization work.

WOMEN IN THE DEPARTMENTS

Fortunately Sir Gerald Bellhouse, a man noted for his justice and fair dealing, became Chief Inspector about that time, and this greatly helped the scheme.

In 1928 another departmental committee was appointed, under the chairmanship of Lieut.-Colonel Sir Vivian Henderson, to consider amongst other matters whether any changes in the organization were desirable. During the seven years in which the new scheme had been in operation complaints had been received (although surprisingly few) in regard to the inspection by women of works where men only or mainly were employed. Hence this was a matter to which the committee gave special attention. "Arrangements have been in force under the reorganization scheme," they reported, "by which works in the heavy industries are generally left to the men inspectors. The representatives of the employers who appeared before us asked for an extension of this arrangement to all works where men only or mainly are employed—particularly works containing engineering and woodworking machinery. In support of this request they referred to the absence among the women inspectors of technical engineering qualifications and an alleged inability to sense the 'works atmosphere,' but the point upon which they laid most stress was that the inspection of these works by women inspectors was not acceptable to the employers and that this 'lack of acceptance' must militate against the results achieved by the women inspectors. We have no evidence, however, to show that this apprehension has been borne out by actual experience, and the employers' representatives did not advance any cases in which the women inspectors had in any way failed in the duties placed upon them since 1921. On the contrary, it was admitted that the women inspectors did not miss anything in their inspections, and the evidence as a whole shows that they have carried out their work with efficiency and zeal. Moreover, the representatives of the Trades Union Congress General Council expressed the view that women inspectors were fully as competent as the men and told us that they did not see any objection at all to women inspectors dealing with works where only men are employed. We understand that the view put forward by the employers' representatives is based chiefly on psychological grounds of a rather vague nature, and we do not feel we should be justified in making it the basis of a recommendation involving a serious departure from the existing system. We anticipate that, as inspection by women inspectors develops, any sentiment of opposition to inspection by women as such will tend to disappear."

The committee made some further important recommendations. With respect to the proportion of women in the inspectorate, they regarded the present number as too small, in view of the amount of the work which was common to both sexes or better suited to women, and in view of the importance of securing a sufficient number of experienced women inspectors. They recommended that the proportion should be increased within the next few years to 30 per cent, and that the method of recruitment should be exactly the same for men and women and that they should be selected by the same board.

Further, they considered that the time had now come to abolish the post of Woman Deputy Superintending Inspector and that the grading of the women inspectors should be assimilated to that of the men inspectors. On the

WOMEN IN THE DEPARTMENTS

other hand, they felt that it was not yet the moment for complete fusion, as it was important in the interests of the service that inspectors of each sex should hold a certain number of the higher posts and that this could only be secured in the case of the women by special arrangement. In order to secure this, the committee recommended that twelve of the posts in the higher grades should be reserved for women, pointing out that, when the recommendation as to the recruitment of men and women had had time to take effect, the balance between the sexes would have attained the proportion considered desirable and it might be found unnecessary to reserve these higher posts. With the exception of the reservation of these posts the committee recommended that the promotions should be upon a basis of common seniority.

Once more in the Factory Department women were given further opportunities of service, involving greater responsibilities and necessitating technical knowledge. In gaining the latter they were helped and encouraged by the broadminded head of the engineering inspectors, Mr. Leonard Ward. In December 1929 Sir John Anderson, Permanent Under-Secretary at the Home Office, told the Tomlin Commission that "undoubtedly the work of the women is quite satisfactory and certainly compares favourably with the work of the men," and that he was in favour of amalgamation of staffs, of recruiting men and women to the same grade in the future and of having the same ladder of promotion.

The recommendations of the Henderson Committee were carried out and, as was predicted, the reservation of posts in the higher grades for women is no longer necessary.

WOMEN SERVANTS OF THE STATE

Men and women are now promoted from the common seniority list, and to-day, in addition to women in the grades of Deputy Chief Inspector and Superintending Inspector, there are eight women in the next highest class and twenty-two women in full charge of districts taking a share with the men of the more important ones.

There have also been further developments. In 1919 a medical woman was appointed on the staff of the Senior Medical Inspector of Factories. She is available for common work and also for any special questions which may arise in connection with the health of women. Women inspectors have on a number of occasions acted as technical advisers to the British Delegation at the International Labour Conference at Washington and at Geneva. In 1928 a woman inspector represented the Home Office at a conference of Directors of Industrial Museums which was held in Berlin. They have sat on departmental committees and have given evidence before commissions and committees and, in short, have taken their share in all the work of the department. This has been made possible by those men officials who, like Mr. Scudamore, have been generous enough to encourage women to render their service. In spite of the Chief Inspector of 1879, the fact has been established that the "sphere of women's work is in the hospital, in the school, in the home," and *also* in the factory.

But it is not only in the Factory Department of the Home Office that there has been a development in women's work. In 1923 the work done in connection with the reformatory and industrial schools and places of detention for young persons and homes approved by the Home Office was centred in what came to be known as the Children's Branch

WOMEN IN THE DEPARTMENTS

of the Home Office. Women inspectors were already employed in connection with this work, and as the years proceeded more were appointed, so that to-day there are two women medical inspectors and three whose primary function is the inspection of the schools and homes provided for women and girls, although they may be called upon occasionally to inspect boys' schools regarding the domestic arrangements. In 1936, when the Probation Branch was established, a woman was appointed as Probation Inspector. Finally, in 1935, the Home Secretary took the course of which Mr. Herbert Gladstone in 1907 was not in favour—he appointed a woman as Assistant Commissioner in the Prison Commission.

MINISTRY OF AGRICULTURE AND FISHERIES

Since 1892, when, as has already been recorded, no one over fifteen years of age was allowed to go near the solitary woman typist, this Ministry has always been shy of employing women. It is true that during the war it had perforce to open its doors to women civil servants, but as soon as possible after the war the doors were kept only ajar. This is surprising in view of the extension of the employment of women in agriculture. After demobilization of the Land Army the post of Woman Adviser to the Department was created, but was "economized" after a brief existence.

In 1920 a woman was appointed to a special post in the Education and Research (Agriculture and Horticulture) Division of the Ministry, which post was later converted into a general inspectorship. Her duties covered the inspection of the agricultural education of women in England and Wales and headquarters work in that connection. In course of time a second woman inspector was appointed with similar duties, and also two women as inspectors of horticulture. In the Fisheries Department of the Ministry a woman has been employed for some years as an assistant naturalist stationed at Lowestoft, while women are eligible as botanists at the Royal Botanic Gardens, Kew.

In 1930 Sir Charles Howell Thomas, Permanent Secretary to the Ministry, informed the Tomlin Commission that it was not possible yet to employ women in certain technical grades, for example as labour branch inspectors, live-stock officers, veterinary inspectors, assistant naturalists and fishery officers. The policy throughout the department was to follow public opinion. "Women are only deemed to be ineligible for those posts where the circumstances in which the work would have to be done would be quite unsuitable to the employment of women, as, for instance, a naturalist going to sea on a fishing trawler; or the environment as, for instance, a wages inspector visiting farms and travelling throughout the country; or a veterinary surgeon, who has to deal with cattle drovers at the ports or with slaughtermen and others during an outbreak of foot-and-mouth disease . . . [or] the live-stock officers [whose] work is in connection with premiums for sires. In every other case all appointments at the Ministry are open to women as well as to men." The witness went on to say that he did not feel the time had come yet to employ women in these posts. To this Lord Tomlin commented: "The point which occurs to me upon that is this, will the time ever come if you do not make a start? . . . It may be one of those things which, unless you begin some time, you never will do it, because it will never be the time. Is there not something to be said

WOMEN IN THE DEPARTMENTS

for the view—I do not quite know how to express it except in a rather flippant way—'Let them all come and take their chance.' . . . Of course it is very difficult to say, but one knows that there are some women who are successful farmers, and there are some women who perhaps are able to induce a more sympathetic hearing than some men, even from the most unsatisfactory audiences."

The result of the deliberations of the Royal Commission was that they recommended in 1931 that the posts of Livestock Inspector, Veterinary Inspector, Labour Inspector, and Secretary to Agricultural Wage Committees should *not* be reserved to men.

Meanwhile women were being increasingly employed in agriculture, and on January 24th, 1932, it was announced in the press that the Executive Committee of the Somerset branch of the National Farmers Union, with a membership of 6,843, the largest in the country, had appointed a woman as secretary of the branch.

On December 11th, 1933, Major Hills asked a question in Parliament on the subject. To this Mr. Walter Elliott replied that the general question of the appointment of women to specialist posts in Government departments was being considered by a central committee (the Committee on Women's Questions already mentioned) and that he would make a further review of the position in due course. Two and a half years later, in June 1936, when asked by Viscountess Astor whether he was now giving effect to the recommendation of the Tomlin Commission, he answered that the whole subject had been considered by the departmental Whitley Council on the report of a committee set up for the purpose; the committee had recommended that the veterinary and live-stock inspectorates should continue to be reserved for men and that the labour inspectorate should be thrown open to both sexes, and this recommendation had been accepted. Lady Astor pointed out that there are at least 50,000 women working regularly on the land, while another member remarked that the committee which made the report were all men. (In this it is probable that he was not strictly correct, and that there was the proportion of the sexes usually found on such committees—a proportion which does not make things easy for the women members.)

BOARD OF INLAND REVENUE AND ESTATE DUTY OFFICE
During the war the Board of Inland Revenue were also obliged to open their doors to women, and they did so widely and thus became accustomed to their employment. In the early post-war days, as a result of their success in the examination, many women became established, and in 1930, in the statement submitted by the Chairman of the Board of Inland Revenue to the Tomlin Commission, he declared that "generally speaking the clerical work of the department affords a minimum of scope for differentiating men's and women's posts. The same is true of higher posts. The sexes are not segregated and there are common seniority lists."

In addition, however, to the women who have found their way into the clerical and executive classes of the Inland Revenue, women are now being employed on other important work for which the Board is responsible, namely, in the tax inspectorate and in the Estate Duty Office.

In 1920 the Chancellor of the Exchequer appointed a committee, under the chairmanship of Sir Warren Fisher, to report on the best method of recruitment to the tax inspectorate, and as a result a scheme of open competitive examinations was instituted, with written papers and an interview. The scheme was supplemented by selection of young members of the general executive class of the Civil Service or analogous classes, nominated as suitable by heads of public departments, and by promotion of young members of the Taxes clerical class. When, in 1924, the tax inspectorate was thrown open to women, these were the methods by which they were recruited, in competition with men. When appointed they were regarded for the first five years of service as cadets, and were required to take the organized course of training provided and to pass the two examinations arranged and conducted departmentally. In 1930 the Chairman of the Board, in his statement to the Tomlin Commission, declared that "there is evidence to show that entrants [to the tax inspectorate] have satisfactorily met the difficulties of the cadet period," and that twenty-eight women were employed. In his evidence there was no suggestion that the women were not equal to the work, the main objection to their employment being that it was wasteful to have to train probationers a proportion of whom would leave for marriage.

Unlike the factory inspectorate, there had been no preliminary years in the tax inspectorate in which women could find their feet before competing with their men colleagues. Young women between twenty-two and twenty-four years of age were all at once plunged into what had for many years been a man's preserve. With mixed universities and the more liberal outlook of younger men, however, the position to-day is very different from what it was in the early days. Since 1924 women have continued to take the open competition for these posts, and many have found satisfaction in the work. There are now twenty women inspectors and sixteen women assistant inspectors of taxes. Every path of life appeals to some women if they have the opportunity of walking in it, and to it they bring their own special contribution.

The Estate Duty Office, like the tax inspectorate, demands a distinct class of work, being specialized to a degree which renders it quasi-professional. In addition to a knowledge of death-duty law, the technical staff must possess an adequate knowledge of a great body of general law. Since 1928 recruits for this office have been taken from the open competitions for the executive group of posts, successful candidates entering as assistant examiners. It is a condition of service, however, that they shall in due course either obtain a university degree in law or be called to the Bar. After the end of five years, assistant examiners who have obtained the necessary legal qualification are given the title of "Examiner" and receive a special salary allowance. Women have found their way into the Estate Duty Office by the same entry as men, and at the present time there are fourteen women examiners, possessing of course the necessary legal qualification, in addition to seventeen women assistant examiners.

OTHER DEPARTMENTS

In a volume of this length it is not possible to do more than touch on many of the other departments into which women have found an entry and where they are rendering their special service.

As has already been recorded, women doctors have for

WOMEN IN THE DEPARTMENTS

many years been employed in some departments. In more recent years women lawyers have also found a footing, and women with legal qualifications are being employed in the Public Trustee Office, the Land Registry, and the Board of Control, as well as the Estate Duty Office.

In the National Savings Committee the Senior Chief Commissioner is a woman, and indeed a married one, her services to the department being too valuable to be dispensed with on marriage.

The Customs and Excise Department, entrusted during the war with the administration of the Old Age Pensions Acts, has continued this work, and a number of women are employed as Old Age Pensions officers and a few as Old Age Pensions surveyors, but they remain more or less segregated. The employment of women as Customs and Excise officials was considered by the Tomlin Commission, and it was argued that it might be desirable to appoint women officials to deal with contraband goods coming into the country, especially through the instrumentality of women. In many countries these posts are filled by women; indeed, most travellers on the Continent—men and women —have had their luggage examined by elderly women at the customs. The Commission, however, declared that they did not think that the time was ripe in this country for the appointment of women officers of Customs and Excise and that these posts should be reserved to men.

The Civil Service Commission, which was one of the first departments to open its doors to the higher grade woman during the war and has treated them with its traditional justice, has appointed a woman as Assistant Director of Examinations. Most of the museums, for example the British Museum, the Natural History Museum, the Victoria and Albert Museum, have women as assistant keepers, doing work similar to that of their men colleagues and having been appointed as the best candidates in an open field of recruitment. Women are also to be found as assistant cataloguers in the British Museum and in the libraries of the India Office and the Board of Education.

In the Department of Scientific Research women are engaged on all kinds of scientific work at the main laboratory at Teddington and also in connection with Forest Products research.

In aviation, women have made and are making great conquests, and, in a speech delivered in London in 1937, the then Director General of Civil Aviation was generous in his appreciation of the services they have rendered in the air. "The pioneer work done by airwomen," he declared, "has been of prime importance in the development of the civil air routes of the world. . . . During the war many women rendered invaluable practical assistance to the Royal Air Force both from their knowledge of actual flying and of aeronautical engineering, and the *esprit de corps* of those days still survives in the annual reunion of survivors." After paying a tribute to the various outstanding flights by women aviators, he continued: "Many women technicians and engineers, although they may not devote their energies entirely to aeronautical engineering, nevertheless have a special interest in that direction, which affords perhaps more than any other class of engineering great scope for individuality and the employment of new ideas." The Air Ministry employs women as technical officers and in other similar posts and undoubtedly the future will see

WOMEN IN THE DEPARTMENTS

a great increase in the employment of women in work connected with this Ministry.

In view of the fact that before the war women motorists were rare, it is of interest to find them employed in the Ministry of Transport as driving examiners, and men have now to resign themselves to being tested by women—whom they often regard as far too conscientious—before they can obtain their driving licences.

The Land Registry employs women as mapping assistants and tracers. The Admiralty also employs women in the latter kind of work, both in Whitehall and in the technical departments at the home dockyards, and a fair number of girls and women have found an outlet for their taste for drawing in this form of employment.

In the Public Trustee Office women have always been employed, and as the years go on their employment has been increased and their scope widened.

"Many reasons are urged," it is pointed out in *Women Workers in Seven Professions*, "for admitting women more freely to a share in the responsible work of the service, but the true basis of their claim lies in this—that the most successful form of government and the happiest condition for the governed can only be attained in the State as in the family when masculine and feminine influences work in harmony." The employment of women in the departments has, indeed, borne this out.

CHAPTER 6

THE MARRIAGE BAR

IN the very early days of women's service to the State the employment of married women was in certain quarters not regarded with disapproval, and the fact that women might marry and leave the service was not held up against them to any great extent as a reason for not employing them. Indeed, Mr. Scudamore, as has already been stated, was of the opinion that the fact that women retired on marriage was for various reasons a definite asset. Everyone who has been in charge of a men's staff must have wished for some similar method of bringing in fresh blood more often. To lose highly trained people on a staff is of course a drawback, but it is a drawback which has often been over-emphasized. There is no such thing as indispensability, and retirements often prove an advantage in many directions. Moreover, the extent of wastage owing to marriage is inclined to be exaggerated, as is shown by the following figures. In the four years ending March 31st, 1934, the average number of women retiring annually for this reason was in all groups less than 4 per cent. In the clerical, writing assistants, and typing classes it varied from 2·5 to 3·4 per cent, while in the executive, inspectorate, and professional and technical groups it was only 1 to 1·4 per cent.

Although Mr. Scudamore did not decry retirement due to marriage, it does not seem to have occurred to him to require such retirement; he realized that the majority of

THE MARRIAGE BAR

women would resign voluntarily. He left them to make the decision themselves or in consultation with their husbands, remarking that "we do not punish marriage by dismissal" and "we encourage married women to return to the service." His view was upheld by Mr. G. R. Smith, of the Returned Letter Office, who told the Playfair Commission that he had a married woman on his staff. He was asked whether "under certain circumstances" leave of absence might be granted as had been done, it was pointed out, in the Telegraph Department, where a case of the kind had occurred. The suggestion does not appear to have astonished Mr. Smith, as, although he admitted he had not heard of the case, he remarked that in such cases he presumed "substitutes would be appointed."

Soon, however, a change came about, owing perhaps to the fact that women were becoming established, and in 1875 the Post Office laid down the rule that "a married woman not being a widow is not eligible for any appointment on the establishment of the Post Office and any single woman now on the establishment who may marry will be required to resign. This rule will not apply to married women now in the service nor to persons who do not hold a regular appointment from the Postmaster-General."

Gradually it was felt that this was a question which must not be left to women to decide for themselves, and so resignation on marriage became generally the rule, although in one or two departments women were allowed to stay on after marriage or no special rule on the subject was made. In any case the matter had become a departmental one.

A petition from the women typists employed in the public service brought the matter to a head. They asked for an increase in their pay and for establishment, and to these requests "My Lords of the Treasury" replied in a minute on March 17th, 1894. Although the class was a small and minor one, the decision in regard to it was to have important consequences, for the minute stated that, although the women typists should be placed on the permanent staff of the Civil Service, with its attendant privileges, *e.g.* a claim to pension, the rule of resignation on marriage should be definitely laid down.

It was fortunate, indeed, for the many thousands of women civil servants in the service to-day that, because some women might marry, "My Lords" did not consider that the remainder should not be entitled to establishment. The minute went on to say that "candidates will be informed that the service of a woman typist ceases as a matter of course on marriage, but it will be open to the head of the department, with the consent of the Treasury, to grant to a typist who marries after a completed service of six years such a gratuity out of the vote for the department as may be agreed upon, not exceeding one month's pay for each completed year of employment as a typist, provided that her character and service are in every respect satisfactory."

It soon became clear that the grant of a marriage gratuity could not be confined to women typists, and in March 1895 the Treasury issued a circular to departments, inviting their views as to the extension of the terms of the minute to all classes of established female labour.

In the following November a minute was sent to departments, extending the grant of marriage gratuities to all classes of established female labour in the public departments, subject to certain conditions, one of these being that

THE MARRIAGE BAR

"the grant of such gratuities will be limited to cases in which resignation on marriage is required by general departmental regulation."

It appears clear from this minute that, prior to it, resignation on marriage was the general, but not the universal, rule. From that time few married women were employed in established posts. The minute, although it did not specifically enjoin resignation on marriage, had the effect of ensuring a fairly general adoption of the practice. Still there were exceptions, as is shown by the Report of the Royal Commission of 1903 on Superannuation in the Civil Service, in which it is stated "the ineligibility of married women as civil servants has not been universally regarded" in the service.

The question was seriously considered by the MacDonnell Commission in 1912, but, as in the case of other questions in connection with the employment of women, the Commissioners were unable to agree. The majority admitted that by the operation of the rule in regard to marriage the service lost the value of a woman's prior training; still, they regarded it as essential to maintain the existing rule intact, and, apart from considerations as to the welfare of the family (which they said must not be ignored), they believed "that the responsibilities of married life are normally incompatible with the devotion of a woman's whole time and unimpaired energy to the public service." Eight signatories to the Majority Report signed a reservation that they were "unable to agree to a hard-and-fast regulation of compulsory retirement on marriage. We believe," they declared, "that there are many cases, especially in the higher grade of work or where women are appointed for highly specialized knowledge, in which the enforcement of this rule would act to the public disadvantage." Apparently they could not go so far as to require either from a man or woman the devotion of the official's "whole time and unimpaired energy" to the public service or to say that the responsibilities of married life are normally incompatible with this devotion.

The position therefore remained unchanged. The departments apparently considered it necessary to make resignation on marriage compulsory for all if the benefit of the marriage gratuity was to be assured for any of their women staff.

When the Government introduced the Sex Disqualification (Removal) Bill into Parliament on October 27th, 1919, the first clause ran as follows: "A person shall not be disqualified by sex from the exercise of any public function, etc." Major Hills immediately moved as an amendment the insertion of the words "or marriage" after the word "sex," pointing out that his object was to ensure that there would be no survival of an ancient law under which the mere fact that a woman is married might disqualify her from an office which otherwise she would be entitled to hold. In his speech he covered the arguments in favour of the removal of the marriage bar. The only grounds on which its continuance might be defended were those of the interests of the State, or of the woman, or of her family. As far as the State was concerned, he contended that, as long as the woman served the State properly, she ought to be entitled to carry on her work after marriage as well as before. If she was a worse public servant because she was married, then let her be displaced for inefficiency. He pointed out that "in private occupations married women

THE MARRIAGE BAR

form the very best servants of their employers." As to the interests of the women themselves, he urged that the rule acted as a deterrent from marriage, and that it was very hard on a woman that she should be put to the very difficult choice either of not marrying a man whom she wanted to marry or of giving up her employment. In regard to the interests of the children, great weight should be given to the views of women themselves on this matter. He had found that all the women's organizations, who certainly had the interests of women and children deeply at heart, supported the removal of the bar.

The Solicitor-General accepted the amendment (being anxious to show that the Bill was a real effort on the part of the Government to meet a difficulty and to fulfil pledges given) on the condition that it would not rule out amendments which he proposed to introduce later on the proviso.

He argued that maternity would interfere with the service of women to the State and that the removal of the marriage bar might be a severe temptation to women to remain childless. Further, it was necessary to consider whether it was in the interests of the children that women should be employed and by that means rendered unable to perform their full service at home. He pointed out that the effect of the proviso which he was introducing would be that regulations would be made, in the interests of the woman and of the State, that she should retire on marriage, subject of course to the receipt of the gratuity.

During the discussion of the proviso, Sir Samuel Hoare contended that on such questions as marriage and childbirth women were just as well qualified to express their opinion as was the Solicitor-General, and that it was essential not

WOMEN SERVANTS OF THE STATE

to leave these questions to Orders in Council or to departments to decide. He pointed out that for several years he had served upon the Royal Commission enquiring into all the departments of the Civil Service, and that practically in every department "one came up against a solid opposition against the entrance of women in any large numbers. If we leave the matter to Orders in Council . . . to decide what are to be the conditions of the entry of women, I am confident they will hedge those conditions around with every kind of restriction and make it impossible for women to enter save in exceptional cases. That to my mind would be a calamity."

The Solicitor-General in reply disagreed with this suggestion that the bureaucracy of the Civil Service were concerned in keeping out women. "I have had an opportunity of consulting with some of those who are in charge of the matter," he declared, "and I have found that they have taken a strong view and insisted as I have done upon the valuable services which have been rendered by women and that they are determined to secure that a good opportunity shall be given to them for employment."

As has already been recorded, the proviso was inserted in the Bill and an Order in Council was made in pursuance of it on July 22nd, 1920, under which special regulations might be made by the Treasury with respect to "the conditions on which women admitted to the Civil Service . . . may be appointed to or continue to hold posts therein." On August 26th, 1921, regulations were made laying down that all female candidates for any established posts in the Civil Service should be unmarried or widowed, and that women holding any such post should be required

THE MARRIAGE BAR

to resign their appointment on marriage, and that under certain conditions they should be entitled to a gratuity. There was, however, a proviso that exceptions might be made on the recommendation of the head of the department, if the Civil Service Commissioners and the Treasury (in cases of recruitment) and the Treasury (in case of an officer already holding an established position) were satisfied that it was in the interests of the public service that such exception should be made.

These regulations were consequent on the Sex Disqualification (Removal) Act and gave for the first time a definite legal basis to what had been a general practice in the service. At the same time they contained a definite suggestion that it might be in the interests of the public service to appoint a married woman or retain her services after marriage.

The regulations were in force when the Tomlin Commission was appointed in 1929 to consider, amongst many other matters, "conditions of retirement from the Civil Service, including the retirement of women civil servants on marriage."

In their report they pointed out that, since the regulations were made, on only one occasion—in March 1931—had use been made of the exception. They found there was considerable divergence of opinion on the subject. All the official witnesses were in favour of the retention of the bar, while a number of outside organizations representing women's interests submitted evidence in favour of its removal. "The balance of organized service opinion," they reported, "is against the removal of the bar in the lower grades, but . . . there is a considerable body of opinion in favour of treating the higher grades differently from the lower grades in the matter."

Amongst the Commissioners also there was a divergence of opinion, although they submitted a unanimous recommendation. The majority held the view that there was weight in the argument that the retention of the marriage bar resulted in the loss to the service of experienced workers, but this applied only to officers in the higher grades. In other grades retirement on marriage resulted in securing a rapid turnover of staff employed on routine duties, and this was an advantage. On balance they felt that the disadvantages which would result from the removal of the bar would outweigh those resulting from its retention, but that the retention could be combined with some provision to meet the objection that by it the service loses experienced workers. The other Commissioners felt strongly that the arguments against the retention of the marriage bar outweighed those in favour, and they would have preferred to make retirement on marriage a voluntary matter. Failing that, and in view of the expressed opinion of the lower grades, who were in favour of the bar, they would have wished to see its removal in relation to all those branches of work for which a higher educational standard is demanded of entrants and in which valuable experience is gained. They would therefore have desired to see the bar lifted as it affects the administrative class, certain specialist classes, and the inspectorates.

Since, however, they desired to go as far as possible with their colleagues, some of whom felt equally strongly on the other side, they agreed to put forward a recommendation on the following lines. The discretionary power should

THE MARRIAGE BAR

become an effective instrument, which so far had not been the case. It was not enough to say that the decision whether a certain person should be retained or appointed to the service ought to be determined by relation to "the interests of the public service," since this might be regarded as, on the one hand, justifying the retention of any officer of average or more than average efficiency, or, on the other hand, as requiring the resignation of any officer who was not irreplaceable. If the discretionary power was to be operative, the manner in which it was to be exercised should be more precisely defined. Although it was undesirable that the discretionary power should be limited in its application rigidly to specific grades, it "should be regarded as specially applicable to the higher administrative staff, to medical officers, factory inspectors, inspectors of schools, and to officers holding research and other posts calling for special qualifications." As to the authority who was to exercise the discretion, the Commission recommended that, on application by the woman concerned, the head of the department and the Treasury (and, in case of recruitment, the Civil Service Commissioners also) after joint consideration should make the exception, if they are satisfied "that appointment to or retention in the public service of a married woman is advisable in the light of her special qualifications or special experience in relation to the duties required of her."

In 1933 the subject was referred to the Committee on Women's Questions. This Committee agreed with the recommendation of the Tomlin Commission, with the addition of the words "or of the special requirements of the department in which she is serving," and they dealt with the question as to how far the Civil Service Regulations for appointment to particular classes should contain a specific reference to the possibility of recruiting or retaining married women.

They made an important recommendation in regard to the question of leave and pay in the event of confinements. Special leave on full pay should be allowed, they considered, for a period not exceeding two months, to be extended up to three months if recommended by medical certificate. This recommendation made it clear that the Committee had in mind the retention of women of child-bearing age.

The reinstatement of married women separated from or deserted by their husbands, or married to men physically or mentally incapacitated, was also dealt with in the Report of the Committee, which was published in 1934.

More and more it became realized that many women have financial obligations which make marriage impossible unless they can retain their position.

Between 1934 and 1938 eight women civil servants have been retained on marriage. The small number is not surprising, for the mesh of the sieve through which their applications have to go is a fine one. It has to be shown that they have special qualifications or special experience in relation to the duties required of them or that there are special requirements in the department in which they are serving. Whether their qualifications and experience and the requirements of the departments are "special" is not easy of determination, and some women have wished that, as in view of the expressed opinion of the lower grades, it would have been unreasonable to make retirement on marriage a voluntary matter, the suggestion supported by some of the

THE MARRIAGE BAR

Tomlin Commissioners had been followed, and that the marriage bar had been retained for the lower grades of the service and removed altogether in regard to the higher grades. By this course women themselves would have settled a matter on which their opinion is peculiarly opportune, and it would not have been left in the hands of authorities who must of necessity have different standards on which they base their decisions.

Still, opinion on the subject appears to be changing, or rather reverting to Mr. Scudamore's view. On February 5th, 1938, *The Times* recorded what they called "a new precedent." The Ministry of Labour in consultation with the Treasury had retained a woman principal in the Ministry on marriage because of the need of her services in the grade. Hitherto permission to remain had only been granted to six women, all in professional, technical, or executive grades, and this was the first administrative woman officer to be so retained. This, they pointed out, marked a new precedent in the administration of regulations governing the employment of married women in the Civil Service.

CHAPTER 7

PAY AND SUPERANNUATION

THE question of the pay of women in the Civil Service would require a volume to itself. It is not proposed to deal with it here at any length, since the main object of this book, as has been clearly indicated, is to show the service women have rendered to the State. Service must of necessity, however, depend on conditions of employment, amongst which the question of pay is an important factor.

In the early days Mr. Scudamore did not attempt to hide his opinion that amongst the advantages which would accrue through the employment of women was the fact that the wages which would "draw male operators from but an inferior class of the community would draw female operators from a superior class," and that they were "less disposed than men to combine for the purpose of extorting higher wages." In short, women were cheap and not, he thought, "association-minded."

There was no doubt about it, they were cheap. In the Telegraph Office they received as operators 8s. a week when first engaged, 20s. at twenty-one years of age, rising gradually to £78 a year; while the men received 12s. to commence with, rising to £160 a year. The women clerks in the various branches of the Post Office received a salary of £65 a year, rising by increments of £3 to £80. When promoted to the rank of first-class clerk they received £85, rising by £5 increments to £110. The opinion was prevalent that women workers lived at home, and hence "pin

PAY AND SUPERANNUATION

money" would suffice. The fact that many of them had to support themselves and even help to support others was often not recognized.

The writer of an article on "Women as Civil Servants" in the *Nineteenth Century* of September 1881, however, realized it and gave publicity to the subject. The article gives a vivid picture of the conditions under which women worked in the "Public Postal Service" and the duties expected of them. He describes, for instance, the Government Account Section, "the highest room [of which]," he says, "is where the Government messages and those of the Queen and her family are counted and charged to the offices and to the controllers of the Royal Households. This apartment is far up above the noise of the streets, and a small balcony allows the clerks to breathe the fresh air from the river. A few withered ferns outside the window struggle to keep life in them, and are carefully tended by their owners, but the smoke and fog do not encourage the growth of young leaves." He goes on to say that "in contrasting the work of the women with that of the men in the Post Office, the authorities say that the women are more conscientious and take a greater interest in their occupation"; this, he considers, is easily accounted for by the class of women employed—ladies. "Many a sad history is connected with their entrance on official life. The young men in the Post Office spend their time in exercise or amusement when the hours of work are over. Many of the women go home to continue their exertions in some other form. The salary is small, and one tries to increase it by giving lessons; another by sewing; a third in drudgery of a domestic kind. The continuous close application is often found a relief from pressing thoughts of great sorrow or loneliness; or there may perhaps be anxiety to rise as rapidly as possible to a higher position in the section, that a larger salary may be obtained. The clerks in some cases have others depending on them. Lodgings, where two idiot brothers are her only companions, is the home of one woman. A solitary attic near London Bridge is the home of another of these clerks. Possibly the women plod more steadily than the men do. At any rate the authorities are satisfied that nothing is wanting among them of quiet, businesslike ways."

He cites an article in the *Quarterly Review* for January, on the "Employment of Women in the Public Service," which draws attention to the rate at which female clerks are paid in the Post Office, and regrets the disparity between their salaries and those of the men. "Less than half the amount of remuneration is received for doing the same work in quantity and quality, and this although the women are now performing a higher class of duties than at the time when the salaries were originally fixed." He enumerates the reasons underlying this apparently unjust disparity. Firstly, the health of the women is not so good as that of the men clerks, which he attributes *inter alia* to the monotonous employment which "seems to wear them a great deal more than it does the other sex," and to the fact "that many bring little or no lunch with them and abstain from ordering food in the building and work hard after office hours." Secondly, there has to be taken into account the cost of the arrangements made for their comfort, for example kitchen fires and cooking and dining halls, "as strict rules forbid the female clerks to leave their apartments from the time they arrive until they depart in the afternoon." "Lastly,

PAY AND SUPERANNUATION

and above all," he says, "the market price of the work is the present rate of payment, and only time can alter the fact. Were all the female clerks to resign in a body, their places would be filled in a few days. The market is overcrowded, and while this remains the case all arguments in favour of an increase of wages fall pointless. It is true forty pounds is too little to live upon, therefore women who cannot afford to wait until they rise to be first-class clerks must seek a livelihood elsewhere. The employment of women is certainly a great saving to the service, but when they were admitted it was for the express purpose of economizing by cheap labour."

The writer of this article had no doubt that women's labour was cheap.

Mr. Scudamore, however, was wrong when he thought they would not combine for the purpose of extorting higher wages. In 1889 Her Majesty's Commissioners on Civil Establishments were the recipients of a document headed "Female Statement" from the Female Clerks (Established) of the Central Telegraph Office, in which they state their position and prospects in respect of pay, privileges, and hours of duty. They conclude their statement as follows:

"In the event of reorganization of the staff being considered, may we beg to submit that a senior class should be formed similar to that of the male staff.

"That on account of the importance of the duties performed, and of the length of service rendered in attaining the maximum of the first class, the salaries and increment should be raised.

"That the scale of pay be as follows:—

"12s. per week on entering the service; 14s. per week

on passing the examination, rising thence by 2s. per week per annum to a maximum of 40s. per week. Senior clerks to commence at £110 per annum, and rise by annual increments of £5 to a maximum of £130 per annum.

"That the official duty should be seven hours per diem.

"That full pay should be granted during sickness.

"That annual leave should be extended to one calendar month after ten years' service.

"That all duty performed on Bank Holidays should be paid for in overtime.

"We respectfully beg that two representatives to be selected by the Female Clerks may be allowed to give evidence on their behalf before your honourable body."

So much for the Female Clerks (Established) of the Central Telegraph Office; in spite of Mr. Scudamore's prognostications they had become "association-minded."

In 1897, at short notice, the women clerks in the other branches of the Post Office received a rude shock—their starting salary was reduced from £65 to £55 rising by increments of £2 10s.—instead of £3—to the maximum of £100. This reduction was probably owing to the creation of the class of men assistant clerks to provide an outlet for the boy clerks, who were required to leave the service at eighteen years unless they found their way into a permanent grade. The assistant clerks' scale was the same as that of the reduced women clerks. The reduction caused a volume of discontent and led to the formation of the first women's association, known as the Association of Post Office Women Clerks. As the years have proceeded, more women's associations have been established, and to-day, in addition to this method of organization, men's associations in the Civil

PAY AND SUPERANNUATION

Service have been opened to women and they have freely entered them.

With the formation of the Association of Post Office Women Clerks, there was now a recognized body to represent women's views before committees, and they made headway. Several women civil servants gave evidence before the Select Committee on Post Office Servants, which was appointed in 1906 under the chairmanship of Mr. Charles H. Hobhouse. A representative of the Female Telegraphists explained that "the whole principle on which the scale of payment of women has been fixed in the past has been that of a pocket-money wage. But what is a pocket-money wage to the few has to serve as a living wage to the many. ... That £1 weekly (the salary now received at the age of womanhood) is wholly insufficient is ... proved by the following table:—

	£	s.	d.
Rent, light and firing		7	6
Board at residence		5	6
Board at office		4	6
Travelling		1	6
Laundry		1	0
	£1	0	0

an annual outlay of £52, no surplus being left for clothing, annual holidays, necessary recreation, possible illness, etc. Thus it will be seen that recreation so urgently needed has to be either considerably curtailed or foregone altogether, and that this, coupled with insufficient or improper food, must invariably lead to the undermining of the health—the continual worry and anxiety consequent upon having to strive to make both ends meet does probably result in additional sick leave. If £1 weekly at twenty-one years of age is insufficient, the whole gravity of the position will be realized when it is stated that the average wage during the first seventeen and a half years of a woman's service is but 25s. weekly. . . . We ask that the remuneration of female telegraph clerks in London shall be £67 16s. on completion of five years' service or twenty-one years of age, and thence rise uninterruptedly by 2s. weekly, or £5 4s. per annum, to a maximum wage of £130 per annum."

Another woman described how a clerk earning from 14s. to 30s. found, even on the maximum, that it was difficult to live in lodgings in London with a reasonable degree of comfort. "She is only just able to pay her expenses, in the ordinary way, and so long as no serious illness overtakes her (for we cannot avail ourselves of the free medical attendance of the Government, unless we are well enough to see the Medical Officer at the Department). She is not able to afford the simplest pleasures with any frequency if she desires to make provision for the annual holiday. There are three types of 'home' open to the woman who has to live on 30s. (or less) per week. These are: (1) The semi-charitable 'Home for Business Ladies'; (2) the furnished room, without board or attendance; (3) the third-rate boarding-house. The average woman chooses the third type, even though the boarding-house she can afford can only be described as third-rate. She will have to share a bedroom with one or two more boarders, who probably are perfect strangers to her, because the majority of boarding-house keepers will not let a woman have the smallest of

PAY AND SUPERANNUATION

bedrooms to herself, unless she is prepared to pay at least 15s. per week. We admit very readily that it does not hurt any woman to pass through a period of her life in experiences such as these. But we do plead that, for a well-educated woman with refined tastes, some degree of intellectual culture, and a natural wish to keep in touch with the society in which she was brought up, who at twenty-nine or thirty years of age has just reached her maximum, the outlook is very depressing and hopeless. The appended table has been worked out in detail, though only the summary is given:—

	£	s.	d.
Board and lodging		14	0
Board at office		4	6
Fares (to and from office)		1	6
Laundry		1	3
Clothing		5	6
All other expenses, including provision for annual holiday		3	3
	£1	10	0

Therefore, in consideration of the reasons given below, we ask that our scale of pay be in future 14s. per week, rising by annual increments of 2s. weekly to £2 10s., and that prospects of promotion be open to us."

A witness from Manchester, after tactfully beginning her statement with the remark, "We women much appreciate the graceful and frank statement made by Mr. Babington Smith with regard to the efficiency and capability of the women employed by the Department," continued: "We would consider it a calamity if the Department deprived us of any of the duties now open to us: we are not complaining because of the responsibility, nor on account of the arduous work; the keynote of our contention is that *we are not paid* for the duties we perform. We have the same punishments and fines as the men; and we think that this shows that we are regarded as being equally responsible. Precisely the same work; implying equal capability. The same hours of duty, the same length of annual leave; showing that we need an equal period of rest and change. The limit of service is the same; for, except in case of ill health, a woman wends her weary way to the age of sixty before she attains full pension. Any woman who has served the Department for over forty years will certainly not trouble the Department long for the pension allotted to her. Equality we have on so many points, and yet the great disparity in wage, anything from 21s. and upwards in the larger offices to 11s. a week in the smaller." (This witness received her reward—when she retired it was from a position of responsibility carrying with it a salary of £600 a year.)

Other women witnesses appeared before the Committee; indeed, by now women seemed as disposed as men "to extort higher wages."

The question of the pay of women civil servants was also considered by the MacDonnell Commission in 1912. "The majority of us," so the report stated, "recommend that in so far as the character and conditions of the work performed by women in the Civil Service approximate to identity with the character and conditions of the work performed by men, the pay of women should approximate to equality with that of men. The evidence which we have received indicates that women's services are (subject to exceptions which in the higher branches are important) less

PAY AND SUPERANNUATION

efficient on the whole than those of men. . . . A considerable proportion, for instance, of women civil servants marry and leave the service before they have reached their full degree of efficiency, and men are, we are told, more likely than women to stand the extra exertion called for at a crisis. In so far as this difference of efficiency exists, the salaries of men should, we believe, remain higher than those of women." The actual difference in salaries did not seem to the Commissioners to result from any general consideration of the problem, and they instanced the case of highly qualified women inspectors receiving salaries little more than one-half of those paid to men inspectors of similar grade employed in the same department. Accordingly they recommended that the Treasury should institute a general enquiry with the object of removing inequalities of salary not based on differences in the efficiency of service. Action on this recommendation, however, was suspended owing to the war.

The practice of granting bonus additions to salaries was started during the war in consequence of the increased cost of living, and gradually remuneration increased, but inequalities of salaries between men and women continued to exist.

After the war the thorny question of women's pay was constantly under review. The Machinery of Government Committee did not offer any recommendations as to the remuneration of women, although expressing the opinion "that no discrimination could properly be enforced merely on the grounds of sex." The Gladstone Committee, although making some recommendations regarding scales of pay for certain posts, did not consider the question of the relative salaries of men and women, which had been referred to the War Cabinet Committee on Women in Industry. This Committee was appointed "to investigate and report upon the relation which should be maintained between the wages of women and men, having regard to the interests of both, as well as to the value of the work." The main finding of this Committee on the general question was that "women doing similar or the same work as men should receive equal pay for equal work in the sense that pay should be in proportion to efficient output. This covers the principle that on systems of payment by results, equal payment should be made to women as to men for an equal amount of work done." This finding, however, was qualified by a recommendation that the question of payment to married men of childrens' allowances should receive careful consideration in connection with payments to teachers to which the Government contribute. As far as the Civil Service was concerned, their most important recommendation was that, if the Treasury enquiry advocated by the MacDonnell Commission had not yet been held, it should be put in hand with the least possible delay.

The Reorganization Committee recommended that women's scales should be related to men's on a recognized and stated basis, and that the minimum of the basic scale in each class should be the same for women as for men, and that the incremental rates should be identical up to a point.

The House of Commons debated the question on May 19th, 1920, under Major Hills' resolution to the effect that it was expedient for women and men in the Civil Service to have equal pay, and again on August 5th, 1921,

PAY AND SUPERANNUATION

when a resolution was passed, "that having regard to the present financial position of the country this House cannot commit itself to the increase in Civil Service salaries involved in the payment of women in all cases at the same rate as men, but that the question of the remuneration of women as compared with men shall be reviewed within a period not exceeding three years." On July 25th, 1923, a further committee reported, under the chairmanship of Sir Alan Garrett Anderson, on the pay and other conditions of employment of State servants. Their report contained a section dealing with women in the Civil Service. Their view is briefly summarized as follows: "In business, it will, in the long run, be satisfactory, both for the employer and for the employed women, to value women by the same standards as men and to give them both the privilege and the burden of economic independence." On this basis "the employer should offer women what is necessary to recruit the type he needs, and to keep his service healthy and efficient. If for the same total cost of pay women do his work better than men, the value of women will appreciate.... If ... for every £ spent on a certain operation a man gives a better return than a woman, that work will tend to be reserved for men. This rule of equal pay for equal value is, we think, not only justice, but the one rule that will permanently satisfy men and women, employers and employed, producers and customers." The committee were inclined to the opinion that as "continuity of service is of distinct advantage ... the young woman should be recruited for administrative, executive and clerical grades at a lower rate than the young man," whereas "as the woman grows older and the risk of marriage decreases, her value in work which requires continuity of service should rise in relation to the value of a man." This is an interesting opinion and one which in time may receive further consideration.

In the years 1924, 1925, and 1929 questions were asked in the House as to the steps taken to give effect to the Resolution of August 5th, 1921, which had asked for a review within three years of the question of the remuneration of women as compared with men. The reply given was that the state of the country's finances made it impossible to justify the great increase in expenditure that would be involved. A request for the appointment of a Committee of Inquiry was also not acceded to, but on April 19th, 1929, the Prime Minister announced to a joint deputation from women's societies that the question of equal pay in the Civil Service would be referred to the Royal Commission on the Civil Service which was to be set up.

Accordingly, in the report of the Tomlin Commission the relations between men's and women's scales were reviewed. The evidence was summarized and the views for and against the introduction of equal pay were given in detail. The conclusion was brief. "We are divided almost equally into those who are not prepared to recommend the introduction of equal pay and those in favour of such a recommendation."

This, then, was the position in 1931, but it was not allowed to remain there for long. Questions in regard to it were asked in the House of Commons, and on June 7th, 1935, the subject was raised on the occasion of the adjournment of the House for the Whitsuntide recess and debated at length without a division being taken. On April 1st, 1936,

PAY AND SUPERANNUATION

in Committee of Supply on the Civil Estimates, on a motion introduced by Miss Ellen Wilkinson, the House affirmed its support of the principle of equal pay for equal work in the Civil Service, by which action the Government was defeated. In a leader in *The Times* on April 3rd we are told: "Though the House of Commons spent an hour yesterday discussing the technicalities of the defeat of the Government on Wednesday, there is really no doubt about what happened or about what is proposed. Technicalities apart, the House of Commons voted against the Government on the question of paying the same wage to men and to women in certain grades of the Civil Service for the same work. This was no snap division. The Government were defeated because thirty-one of their supporters voted with the Opposition and because many others abstained from voting at all. It is safe to say that the general feeling among their supporters was that, though they did not want the Government defeated, they could not endorse an unequivocal negative to this particular question. The second fact in Wednesday's story is that, within a few minutes, on another division the original verdict was reversed, not because more members voted for the Government but because a few less were unwilling to inflict upon them a second defeat. It is impossible to deny that the view of the House was in favour of equal pay for equal work".

Four days later *The Times* reported: "The Government obtained their vote of confidence in the House of Commons yesterday by an enormous majority; but it is only fair to add that they obtained it for reasons more comprehensive than the merits of the question upon which they asked for it, and there was an undercurrent of resentment among some of their supporters that they should have been asked to give a vote which might conceivably be taken to imply a refusal of equal pay for equal work in the Civil Service irrespective of the sex of the worker. . . . The success of the Government yesterday was indeed proof that nobody wants to weaken their hands at a moment of grave international tension."

Meanwhile the claim for equal pay was gaining adherents in the associations of men civil servants. At a meeting of the National Whitley Council held on March 8th, 1935, a request was made by the staff side that a committee should be set up to consider and report upon the existing differences in the pay of men and women civil servants and the changes, if any, which should be made. This was done, the committee consisting of twelve men and five women, and an agreed report was issued on June 30th, 1937. In this report "the staff side of the committee made it clear at the outset that they adhered to the principle of equal pay for men and women in the Civil Service, and that anything which they proposed to do on the committee must be regarded as entirely without prejudice to their views on that principle. They recognized, however, that the official side were not prepared to discuss the question of equal pay, on the ground that it was one of Government policy, and, while indicating that they would pursue their claim wherever and whenever possible, they agreed, as far as the proceedings of the committee were concerned, to confine their aim to adjusting anomalies and lessening differentials within the system as it stands at present." Subject to this reservation the committee was agreed that in regard to grades where there is common recruitment of men and

PAY AND SUPERANNUATION

women, and where common conditions of employment obtain, certain provisions should apply, the most important of which were as follows: "The differentiation between the men's scale and the women's at the maximum shall not exceed 20 per cent; in other words the maximum of the women's scale shall not be less than 80 per cent of the maximum for men in the same grade. . . . In the case of two grades where the men's scales touch or where there is a gap between the men's scales, the maximum of the women's scale shall not be less than the maximum of the men's scale in the grade below. . . . The differential between the men's and the women's maximum in any case shall not exceed £175. . . . In the case of recruitment grades which form the lowest tier of a class and in which the recognized method of filling vacancies is by appointment at the minimum of the scale of candidates at or shortly after the age at which they acquire the prescribed academic or professional qualification, that minimum shall be the same for the men's and the women's scale." Effect is now being given to these recommendations.

This, then, is the position up to date of the vexed question of women's pay in the Civil Service. The authorities are no longer the recipients of a "Female Statement" on the subject but of a statement drawn up jointly by men and women in various grades of the Civil Service, men and women combining "for the purpose of extorting higher wages" for women. How astonished Mr. Scudamore would have been!

As regards superannuation, the position, when the Tomlin Commission was appointed, was that established women civil servants received, under the Superannuation Act of

WOMEN SERVANTS OF THE STATE

1859 amended by the Act of 1884, a pension of one-sixtieth of salary for each year of service, subject to a maximum of forty-sixtieths. Men, on the other hand, under the Acts of 1909 and 1914, received a pension of one-eighteenth of salary for each year of service, plus a lump sum (called an additional allowance) of one-thirtieth of salary for each year of service, subject to maxima of forty-eightieths and forty-five thirtieths respectively.

In 1909 associations of women civil servants asked that women should remain under the Act of 1859. It is said that there were two reasons which influenced women at that time to favour this course; first, that women's salaries were then so low that they could not afford any diminution in the rates of pension calculated on the basis of those salaries, and secondly, that it was feared that if women came under the terms of the new Act the marriage gratuity might be abolished. Twenty years later, however, the position had somewhat changed. The staff side of the National Whitley Council, after ascertaining the views of the women concerned, submitted to the Tomlin Commission that existing established women civil servants should be given the option of coming under the Act of 1909 and that all new entrants should come under it. The women's associations were not unanimous, however, on this subject. The Commission recommended "that existing established women civil servants should be given an option of coming under the Acts of 1909 and 1914 . . . upon terms similar to the terms applicable to the men's option in 1909."

In 1932 a committee set up under the National Whitley Council reported in favour of this recommendation, with the addition that women entering the established service in

PAY AND SUPERANNUATION

future should be brought under the Act of 1909 in the same way as men entering after September 20th, 1909, had been brought under it. Effect was given to these recommendations in the Superannuation Act of 1935. Men and women, therefore, have now the same pension rights.

CHAPTER 8

THREE OUTSTANDING PERSONALITIES

THIS book would be incomplete without honourable mention of some of the women civil servants who helped by their work and example to make it clear that women had a contribution which they could render to the State. During the space of nearly seventy years there have of course been a number of such outstanding women. Many of these are fortunately still living, and it would be invidious to select individuals from amongst them for special mention. Accordingly the following biographical sketches have been confined to three representative women who have run their race and finished their course.

MISS M. C. SMITH

Maria Constance Smith, who in her twenty-third year was chosen as Superintendent of the women newly introduced into the Savings Bank department of the Post Office, came of a scholarly family. Her father, Philip Smith, a well-known scholar and writer, was professor of classics and ecclesiastical history at Cheshunt College and New College. He retired in 1860 and spent the remainder of his life in literary work, contributing to the *Quarterly Review* and other publications edited by his elder brother, Sir William Smith, the lexicographer.

Maria Constance was one of the younger members of a large family, consisting of seven sons and three daughters. She was educated at home by governesses under her father's

THREE OUTSTANDING PERSONALITIES

supervision; she often referred to the personal interest he took in the education of all his children. She had no regular employment before she went to the Savings Bank in 1875, but she assisted her father in looking up references, etc., and similar work, and she continued to live with him at Putney until his death in 1885. She was tall and of good presence and always dressed well. Although she was young when called upon to assume command, the conditions of her early life had tended to develop self-reliance and independence of thought and action. She possessed qualities that go to make a successful ruler and took up her work with the confidence that comes from inherent capability and the courage that does not recognize failure. She realized from the first what civil servants have been slow to realize, that the training of staff is a matter of supreme importance. "Efficiency" was her watchword, and the force of her dominant purpose and magnetic personality was brought to bear to ensure that the women under her control should become efficient. She felt this could best be accomplished by the supervision of the women by their own sex, and undoubtedly in those early days the policy was a wise one. Her sound judgment was shown in her selection of supervising officers, whom she inspired with her own high standards. From the first she insisted on the strict application of service regulations and that no concessions should be granted to women as such. Undoubtedly her regime was a strict one, but if it could have been shown that women were not efficient they would never have kept a footing in the department.

Although she was not inclined to suffer fools gladly, she was never afraid to proclaim her faith in the abilities of her staff. She was convinced that a woman, given similar chances in clerical work, was able to equal a man's output with efficiency. She was careful herself to preserve great independence and would not readily accept the assistance of her men colleagues. On the other hand, in conversation she was vivacious and ingratiating and had an excellent gift of stating her case in a convincing manner and of arousing the interest of the men whose co-operation and influence were vital to the success of her plans for the progress of women. She had no prejudice against the opposite sex; indeed, she liked the society of men. In this connection it may be remarked that, although such a firm believer in the capacity and qualities of women, she never attached herself to any feminist movement.

Mr. Henry Fawcett was wont to say that he considered the head of the women's staff of the Savings Bank one of the ablest officials in the postal service.

She created an impression of greatness in the minds of those brought into contact with her; she made for herself a unique position; all official approach to the women's branches was through her, and she carefully built up what almost amounted to a separate establishment in which she was supreme. She always preserved a very formidable dignity, and she took care to retain it. The Controller and his assistants did not summon her to an interview, they asked her if it would be convenient to receive them; and when on rare occasions she paid a visit to the working-rooms for any special reason she was usually accompanied by some officers of her personal staff. She is said to have disliked the limelight, considering it bad form, and so took care to guard herself from publicity. It was a matter of comment that she made a point of avoiding any public function of a nature which demanded the attendance of the higher officials. This was no doubt sound policy, since her men colleagues were not anxious to advertise the presence of a woman amongst them, and Miss Smith, by absenting herself, was spared the humiliation of finding herself in a less prominent position than was her due in view of her services and the large staff under her control. How accurately she gauged the feeling was evident when the Savings Bank celebrated its jubilee at the Guildhall in 1911. No seat on the platform had been allotted to the woman who had done so much to build up the Savings Bank, and only at the last moment was she remembered and sought out and asked to fill an inconspicuous place. (On the seventy-fifth anniversary of the Savings Bank, at a luncheon at the Guildhall, one woman took her place with the Assistant Controllers and a large number of men civil servants and was presented to the Lord Mayor.)

Yet her services did not go entirely unrecognized. In 1902, on the recommendation of Sir George Murray, the then Secretary of the Post Office, the I.S.O. was conferred on her for her exceptional public services. This was a mark of great distinction and until 1916, when the Order of the British Empire was founded, she held the position of being almost the only woman on whom an honour had been conferred. (In view of the value attached in the Civil Service to recognition of this kind, it is interesting to record that of the present-day women civil servants, a few are C.B.E.'s, more are O.B.E.'s and still more are M.B.E.'s.)

In 1913 she retired after thirty-seven years' service, a reception being given in her honour at Burlington House,

WOMEN SERVANTS OF THE STATE

by the courtesy of the First Commissioner of Works and the Civil Service Commissioners, where a distinguished gathering assembled to show their appreciation of her work. She spent her last years at Folkestone, where she died in 1930 at the age of seventy-seven. She had devoted herself to her life work with a characteristic intensity of purpose. She secured for women civil servants a status and recognition for which they owe her a lasting debt of gratitude. She laid a solid foundation in the Civil Service on which women have been enabled to build.

MISS M. H. MASON

Unlike Miss M. C. Smith, who began her responsible duties at the age of twenty-three, Miss Mason was more than forty years old when she started her official career. She was born in 1845 and was reared in the Victorian tradition at her country home at Moreton Hall in Nottinghamshire. It was due to her early life in the country that her taste for botany and horticulture was developed. Indeed, she was a skilled botanist and excelled also in painting water-colour pictures of flowers. Pursuits, however, of such a gentle nature did not entirely satisfy her. She was vigorous and versatile and soon turned her attention to social problems, in which she became intensely interested.

She became voluntary supervisor of the boarding-out of Poor Law children within all the unions of Nottinghamshire, Vice-President for Nottinghamshire of the Girls' Friendly Society Poor Law Department, and central head of the Young Men's Friendly Society Poor Law Department.

It was not surprising that it was to Miss Mason, with her knowledge and great energy, that Mr. Arthur Balfour

THREE OUTSTANDING PERSONALITIES

turned when he decided to appoint a woman inspector to ascertain whether the regulations under the Boarding-out Order were observed. She thus became an official in 1885 and for twenty-five years carried on her work with unabated enthusiasm and practical good sense. Like many of the women of those days, she had great courage and was not restrained by official considerations from expressing herself on occasions with vigour and terseness. The welfare of the child was her first consideration and she never spared herself in this cause. The fact that child life figures now so largely in social legislation and in the conscience of the nation is no doubt largely due to her untiring work.

In 1901, after seventeen years of continual hard work, she was forced to take sick leave, and in the following year we have her quaintly reporting in her annual report: "This temporary breakdown was due to long and continued overwork, but, lest it should be thought that a woman's strength is not equal to the work of official inspection, I think it right for the sake of women generally to state that since my appointment in 1885 I have only availed myself of the leave of absence to which the inspectors are entitled in seven years out of the seventeen years. The Board have always been most kind in granting me my leave of absence for which I have asked and at any time. My sole reason for taking so little holiday has been that my heart has been in my work and when one urgent call succeeded another without interval I could not but respond."

In 1910 she retired under the age limit and was presented with her portrait and an address by Boarding-out Committees, Boards of Guardians and individual admirers. She did not, however, settle down to a life of idleness; she was far too energetic for that. She went to Africa and travelled widely in that country from Table Mountain to Uganda, and during that time turned to the pursuit of her youth, the painting of flowers in water-colour. All the flowers were natural species and were gathered and painted on the spot and form a valuable record of a botanist. Indeed, in 1916 an exhibition of them was opened in London by Mr. Schreiner, the High Commissioner for South Africa, when it was announced that Miss Mason intended to leave them in her will to the Kew Museum. They now hang in Cambridge Cottage, Kew.

She had a keen appreciation of the beautiful in music and the drama, and was a lively talker and a witty raconteuse.

She published a collection of traditional nursery rhymes and country songs as well as pamphlets and articles on botany, horticulture, and Poor Law. Although a devout churchwoman, she nevertheless interested herself in occult phenomena and was a member of the Psychical Research Society.

Miss Mason spent her last years in South Africa and died there on April 7th, 1932, at the age of eighty-seven. She will always be remembered as a champion of children's rights and as a vigorous and forcible personality.

DAME ADELAIDE ANDERSON, D.B.E.

Dame Adelaide Anderson was another of the band of women who had the opportunity of doing pioneer work; or perhaps it was due to her pioneering qualities that work of this nature came her way. She belonged to a family well known for these very qualities. They were shipowners with

THREE OUTSTANDING PERSONALITIES

a world-wide reputation, great travellers, broadminded, and with far-seeing views.

Adelaide Anderson was born in Australia in 1863 and was the eldest daughter of a large family which returned to England while she was still a child. At first she was educated by a governess at home and then at a school in Dresden, after which she became a student of Queen's College, Harley Street. At the age of twenty she went up to Girton College, where she read moral science and took the tripos in that subject. On coming down from Cambridge she coached girls for examinations, while lecturing at intervals to members of the Women's Co-operative Guild. This work gave her an insight into the conditions of women in industry, a subject in which she became intensely interested, with the result that in 1892 she joined the staff of the Royal Commission on Labour. Her outstanding ability was soon realized, and in 1894 she was appointed by Mr. Asquith as one of the first four women Inspectors of Factories. Thus began the first part of her life's work, which lasted until 1921. In 1897, on Mrs. Tennant's retirement, she was appointed head of the Women's Branch of the Factory Department. Her work in connection with dangerous trades, employment of women and young persons, welfare, legal proceedings, as well as her annual reports, all show her masterly mind, wide knowledge, and length of vision. During the war period, when the women's branch was increased and developed, her genius for seizing new opportunities and her originality of outlook found free play. Like Miss Smith of the Post Office, she had a high standard of efficiency and would not brook second-class work, either in herself or her staff. She built up a women's branch which had the reputation for good work.

The book which she published soon after her retirement in 1921—*Women in the Factory: An Administrative Adventure*—admirably summarizes her work of twenty-eight years and not only her own work, but that of her women colleagues, whose contributions she was always generous in acknowledging.

After her retirement a new life opened itself before her. She visited South Africa, Australia, New Zealand, and Burma, and was then invited to study labour conditions in China. Thus began her great interest in that country. She became a member of the Commission on Child Labour appointed by the Municipal Council of Shanghai in 1923, and published in 1928, under the title of *Humanity and Labour in China*, a documented account of the work of the Commission and its sequel. In 1925 she was appointed a member of the Advisory Committee of the Foreign Office on the Boxer Indemnity Fund and re-visited China with the Willingdon Mission in 1926. Five years later she served on the mission from the International Labour Office to Nanking regarding a factory inspectorate for China, and she was a member of the Universities China Committee in London, 1932–33. It is not surprising that Sir Thomas Wilford, in an account of an interview with her, observed that she had a high place in the hearts of the people of China and that she was always welcome at the Chinese Embassy in London. She admired and understood the Chinese and they admired and understood her.

But it was not only China which she whole-heartedly served; in 1930 she set out alone to Egypt to make enquiries

THREE OUTSTANDING PERSONALITIES

into the conditions of child labour in that country, and her report on the subject, which has been described as a most moving human document, had far-reaching consequences. This journey called to a marked degree for the display of that courage, tenacity and persistence in face of difficulties which never failed her.

South Africa claimed her again, and in 1936, a few months before her death, she returned from a visit to that country which she had undertaken at the age of seventy-two.

Her outstanding qualities are difficult to describe, for she had the mind of a philosopher, coupled with a youthful, eager outlook. She was full of a desire to explore and had an intense power of enjoyment. It is understandable that an article in the *Cape Times* in 1922 called her an "enchanted visitor," and that the reporter who interviewed her on board ship when she arrived was met with the remark, "I never thought anything could be so exquisitely beautiful as Table Mountain and the Bay was at dawn this morning." She always wanted those near her to share with enthusiasm her interest of the moment, and was not always conscious of the fact that they had no desire to do so. Indeed, her strong personality made her at times misunderstood. Children, however, usually understood her; they appreciated her fair-mindedness and power of enjoying the simple pleasures of life. Working women, too, appreciated and always remembered her.

She was a wide reader, a musician, a lover of the arts and a skilful needlewoman. She was also very sociable, she loved parties and bringing her friends together and took pains in regard to their entertainment, especially perhaps in the choice of the wines she offered them.

WOMEN SERVANTS OF THE STATE

Above everything, however, she displayed courage and, although small and fragile in appearance, possessed great powers of endurance and an indomitable determination. Indeed, she had the spirit of a crusader. When her life comes to be written, it will be written because her personality was one which cannot be forgotten.

CHAPTER 9

FUTURE OPPORTUNITIES OF SERVICE

"IF anything conclusive could be inferred from experience," said that wise philosopher, John Stuart Mill, "it would be that the things which women are not allowed to do are the very ones for which they are peculiarly qualified." His pronouncement is borne out by the history recorded in this book. It is probable that the future also will bear it out, for there is still a great service which women are not allowed to render and one for which they may be peculiarly suited. They are not allowed to serve the State in any of His Majesty's possessions overseas or in any foreign country.

THE DIPLOMATIC AND CONSULAR SERVICES

The proviso to the Sex Disqualification (Removal) Act, 1919, which provoked such a lively discussion in the House of Commons, had made it possible for an Order in Council to authorize regulations to be made providing for and prescribing the mode of admission of women to the Civil Service of His Majesty . . . and giving power to reserve to men any branch of or posts in the Civil Service in any of His Majesty's possessions overseas or in any foreign country. An Order in Council was made on July 22nd, 1920, followed by Regulations made by the Civil Service Commissioners with the approval of the Lords Commissioners of His Majesty's Treasury on August 23rd, 1921. These were as follows:—

WOMEN SERVANTS OF THE STATE

1. (On behalf of the Secretary of State for Foreign Affairs.) "All posts in the Diplomatic Service and in the Consular Service are reserved to men. . . ."

4. (On behalf of the Secretary of State for Foreign Affairs and the President of the Board of Trade.) "All posts in the Commercial Diplomatic Service and the Trade Commissioner Service are reserved to men provided that this reservation is not applicable to the post of Chief Clerk in the respective offices of His Majesty's Trade Commissioners."

Thus in 1921 it was decided that women were not to be allowed to serve the State outside this island. The reason for this prohibition puzzled many people. They were aware that service overseas had appealed to women for many generations. Numbers had spent their lives as missionaries in the most remote parts of India and China and the Far East without the prestige of Government service behind them. As doctors, educationalists, nurses, anthropologists, geologists, and explorers, they had lived in some of the most out-of-the-way parts of our colonies. They had been amongst the earliest emigrants to our Dominions. Journeys overseas held no terrors for Dame Adelaide Anderson, and Miss Mason travelled all over Africa painting her pictures of wild flowers. Foreign countries are visited by numbers of young women, often travelling alone or in couples, and visiting, not frequented health resorts, but remote country places. Flying has especially appealed to women. They have, indeed, never shown themselves backward in going overseas when opportunity made it possible and advisable. But still it was felt that women's official services in this direction must be barred.

In 1930 the whole question came up for consideration

FUTURE OPPORTUNITIES OF SERVICE

by the Tomlin Commission, and evidence for and against the admission of women to these services was presented.

On the one side, it was pointed out that women had the same opportunities as men for acquiring the knowledge required for posts of this character, since they could specialize in such subjects as modern history, languages, economics, and international relationships. As regards the personal qualities necessary for such work, they were to be found in some women as in some men. Women were equally concerned with men that foreign affairs should be well administered. Although it had been suggested that to appoint a woman in the Diplomatic or Consular Service might embarrass the country to which it was proposed to accredit her, many countries were now, in international affairs of all kinds, accustomed to the co-operation of women to a considerable extent. They had been sent out as delegates, substitute delegates and technical advisers to the Assembly and the International Labour Conference at Geneva. Further, a fair number of countries had appointed women to diplomatic and consular posts, and work of an exceptionally difficult diplomatic character had been carried out by Miss Gertrude Bell in Mesopotamia and the Arabian Peninsula and had earned the highest commendation. The history of diplomacy and of royal families showed that women had no lack of ability in diplomatic affairs. (Certainly many of the royal ladies of Great Britain have shown an adventurous spirit in travel and a real understanding of foreign relationships.) In regard to the Commercial Diplomatic and Trade Commissioner services, it was pointed out that women were taking a share now in commerce, and

WOMEN SERVANTS OF THE STATE

that several countries were making use of them as Trade Commissioners and advisers on trade matters.

On the other side, Sir Hubert Montgomery, Assistant Under-Secretary for Foreign Affairs, stated quite definitely that he did not think it would be in the public interest to appoint women to diplomatic or consular posts and that he did not consider "they could do their job in posts abroad." He was of the opinion that women would find it very hard to discuss questions and find out things connected with politics and commercial and economic matters and so on, "a great deal of that being necessarily done over *tête-à-tête* meals and in clubs and on occasions of that sort." This witness, however, apparently did not hold diplomacy to be quite outside the province of women, for he said, "we are fully cognizant . . . that the wives of diplomatists can play a very large and important role, and do so—we take our hats off to them—but that, in our view, is largely a matter of team work, it is supplementary to the work of the head of the mission or of the consular officer."

He felt that it would be difficult to employ women in consular posts, especially at ports. "There they have to deal with sailors who are not always quite sober, and who come to the offices of the consul with various grievances, and, if they are not met, they are very apt to become violent and abusive. The sort of grievances they come in with are complaints about their treatment on board ship or the food or the captain's refusal to pay them off before the end of the voyage, and various things of that sort." Undoubtedly many women have had to deal with problems of this kind; a drunken husband, a husband who complains about his

FUTURE OPPORTUNITIES OF SERVICE

food or about his treatment in the office, is no uncommon experience.

The Permanent Secretary to the Treasury, Sir Warren Fisher, took a different standpoint. "I do not know," he said, "that his [Sir Hubert Montgomery's] views and mine at all agree on this topic. . . . I think he takes too gloomy a view. I see no reason why a diplomat should not be a woman in the countries where it is customary to regard women with civility and courtesy." Asked whether the opening of the Diplomatic Service to women was not a question of rather high policy, he replied, "Yes; but it is the same idea, mark you, as inside the country." As to the possibility of difficulties arising owing to the fact that it would not be possible to send a woman diplomat to many countries, he declared: "Of course one can magnify difficulties or one can minimize difficulties. It would be an inconvenience, I agree, but everything new is an inconvenience." In regard to the Consular Service, he said: "I should certainly have women [there] too, but experimentally and quietly. To bring down a guillotine and to say it is impossible for women to do this work is, to my mind, absolute nonsense."

The Tomlin Commission found themselves unable to express a definite opinion on the matter. "In our view," they reported, "the question whether women should be admitted to these services raises issues of high policy which can only be determined by Your Majesty's Government. We note that this matter was reviewed by them at the time of the passing of the Sex Disqualification (Removal) Act. We think that the question should not be regarded as settled for all time by the decision then reached. Having regard to the time which has since elapsed, we recommend that Your Majesty's Government should again examine the position at an early date."

In July 1934 this recommendation was carried out, and an Inter-departmental Committee on the Admission of Women to the Diplomatic and Consular Services was appointed by the Foreign Secretary to review the question, under the chairmanship of Sir Claud Schuster. The committee was composed of representatives of the Foreign Office, the Treasury and the Civil Service Commission, and of two women civil servants of senior rank. The committee met on ten occasions and heard evidence from forty witnesses. In their report, after an historical summary of the matter and a short description of the Diplomatic Service, they set out the arguments which had been addressed to them for and against the admission of women to this service.

The arguments in favour of the admission of women were briefly as follows:—

(a) That, as the general policy in regard to the employment of women is "a fair field and no favour," those who desire to maintain a reservation should show "good cause for making or, when (as in this case) it is already imposed, retaining it."

(b) That women have proved capable of discharging duties of all kinds which some years ago would have been thought impossible of performance by them and, "in particular, duties analogous in kind to those discharged by the Diplomatic Service."

(c) That the value of the work done by women in con-

nection with the League of Nations is "an indication of their aptitude for the work of diplomacy."
(d) That to open the service to women is to increase the field from which candidates could be taken and thereby improve the quality of the service.
(e) That women have a peculiar contribution of their own to make to any kind of work, and particularly to the work of diplomacy. In many countries there are signs that the "women's movements" influence policy. It was claimed "that women rather than men are likely to be able, through their contact with women's societies, to discover more readily what is going on and to appreciate it [the influence of women's movements on policy] at its true value."
(f) That women are employed by foreign Governments in diplomatic positions, which shows that women could do work of this nature, and that in certain foreign countries there would be no obstacle to the employment of British women for this purpose.
(g) That generally speaking "the objections to the admission of women to the service are based in part on prejudice, and in part on fear of the unknown. Similar arguments have been used in the past to justify the exclusion of women from every kind of service, both public and private, and have been proved by experience to be baseless. There may be certain difficulties peculiar to this particular service, but there is no reason to suppose that they will prove insuperable. No doubt the first few women employed abroad will encounter obstacles, and will be looked upon with curiosity by the inhabitants of the country

in which they are appointed to serve. But this will pass away."

On the other side it was argued:—

(a) That it is doubtful "whether the average woman, entering by competitive examination, would now be as efficient as the average man at the average post. . . . The Diplomatic Service is . . . a unified service every member of which must be prepared to go everywhere when called upon. . . . There are countries where the social habits, the political conceptions and the religious beliefs . . . are so fundamentally different from those prevailing in this country that women are not, at least as yet, regarded in a light which would make it possible for them to be employed as diplomatic officers. . . . The employment of women in these countries would not increase and in some cases would definitely decrease the influence of the British mission accredited to them."

(b) That "the introduction of a woman diplomatic officer into the very intimate life of missions abroad would cause difficulties . . . a young woman would not easily fit into the part. It would not be easy to exercise over her the discipline at present exercised over the junior secretaries employed there."

(c) That "work in a British mission abroad must from time to time involve long hours, great strain and anxiety. Many missions—particularly some of the smaller ones—are situated in capitals in very hot climates. Some few capitals are situated at altitudes so great as to impose a strain upon health. The

FUTURE OPPORTUNITIES OF SERVICE

physical constitution of women is not such as to enable them to bear the strain of continuous overwork in hot and unhealthy climates."

(d) "That there are so many posts to which women could not be sent, that certain parts of the world—and those perhaps the most desirable from the point of view of social amenity—would tend to be reserved for women ... as from the time when women had entered the service in any number. Such a condition of things would make the working of the official machine impossible."

(e) That the contribution which women are particularly fitted to make is now adequately performed by wives and daughters of members of the Service without any cost to the State.

(f) That the entrance of women into the Service would involve disturbance and at first certain loss of efficiency and that it is not worth while incurring this unless there is a strong probability that women would present themselves in sufficient numbers to the examination and achieve success in it in reasonable number. The experience in the Home Civil Service shows this is not likely to be the case. (The results of the examinations in 1936 and 1937 may be regarded as negativing this view.)

The Committee were unable to reach any agreement. Four members held that the arguments against the admission of women definitely outweighed those in favour, and therefore recommended no change in the existing position; the two women members took a contrary view, and recommended that women should be eligible for admission on the same terms as men; while the two remaining members were in favour of admitting women for a limited period as an experimental measure.

With respect to the Consular Service, the Committee reported that the general tenor of the evidence was similar to that given regarding the Diplomatic Service. After a discussion of the circumstances which differentiated the two Services they summed up by stating that, with the exception of the two women members, they were agreed "that it would be inadvisable to admit women to the Consular Service." The recommendations of the two women members on this subject were included in an addendum in which they gave reasons for their view.

The Report was submitted to His Majesty's Government, who published it in 1936, together with a statement, in which they declared that they were "convinced that the time has not yet arrived when women could be employed either in the Consular Service or in the Diplomatic Service with advantage to the State or with profit to women." "In taking their decision," they explained, "it must not be thought that His Majesty's Government was questioning the advantage of the employment of women in the Home Civil Service. On the contrary, they fully recognized the services rendered by women in the Civil Service in this country and the advantages which have accrued to the service by their admission to it."

Many persons hope that it will not be long before it is possible to express the same opinion in regard to the service rendered by women in the Diplomatic and Consular Services. After the war of 1914–18, as has been shown,

FUTURE OPPORTUNITIES OF SERVICE

women were employed with advantage in nearly all departments of State. It is hoped that it need not be a case of history repeating itself, and that it will not be necessary to wait for another war before the country can have the advantage of the services of women overseas.

THE COLONIAL AND DOMINIONS OFFICES

The regulations which were made on August 23rd, 1921, also reserved to men all posts in the government services of the Colonies and Protectorates to which appointments are made in the United Kingdom, other than posts for which women may be specially recruited. As it was the practice to send young men officers in the Colonial Office abroad for a certain period and as women were not allowed to serve His Majesty overseas, it had become the custom not to employ women in an administrative capacity in the Colonial Office at home. Further, in view of the fact that there is interchangeability of administrative staff between the Colonial Office and Dominions Office, the practice had arisen of not employing women in an administrative capacity in this latter office also.

This question came also before the Tomlin Commission. It was pointed out by Sir Samuel Wilson, Permanent Under-Secretary for the Colonies, that it would be very embarrassing to have women on the administrative staff of the Colonial Office in view of the fact that they would be under an obligation to do two tours of duty abroad. His objection against employing women in administrative posts was based mainly on this liability to serve overseas. He admitted, indeed, that he did not think the average woman at the present time was as good as a man, but he added,

WOMEN SERVANTS OF THE STATE

"I am not saying what they will be in ten or fifteen years' time." (Half of this period has now elapsed.) . . . "Of course there are some women who are very much better than most men, but I am rather diffident about putting that view."

In the statement he prepared for the Commission, he showed the growth in the sphere of colonial administration. "There has developed, in recent years," he pointed out, "a new sense of responsibility for the welfare and education of the native peoples; and it is now a truism that the duty of trusteeship is the guiding principle of colonial administration. To a large extent the services which at home are supplied by private or municipal enterprise fall to be carried on in the oversea dependencies by the local governments themselves. With the increased resources now available these services are continually extending, not only in connection with the material improvement of life, the preservation of peace and order and improved medical arrangements, but in the provision of education for all races, the study of social anthropology, the revival or protection of native forms of culture, and every activity which can promote moral and intellectual progress. This has resulted in a tremendous increase in governmental activities both at home and oversea, and also in much closer touch being maintained with international movements for the protection and advancement of backward races by co-operation amongst the great colonial Powers, a matter in which the League of Nations has displayed great interest and activity."

The view has been held that many of these questions would seem to be the very ones in which the services of women are needed in an administrative capacity. The

FUTURE OPPORTUNITIES OF SERVICE

Colonial Empire contains a population of nearly fifty millions, of whom probably more than half are women and children, and there must be many problems especially affecting them which could well be dealt with by women. Indeed this witness recognized this fact, for, when asked whether he was suggesting that there was no useful work for women to do in any of the tropical countries, he replied: "Most certainly not. Women are doing magnificent work in various walks of life in the colonies at the present moment as missionaries and in the educational and medical services." In regard to the latter, he admitted that some were actually servants of the Government and that there were a "good many" women doctors in the colonial service.

It was obvious, therefore, that women could and did go overseas in many capacities. Why they should not go in the administrative services evidently puzzled some of the Commission, as is shown by the following questions which were put to the witness:

"(Q) Could you make clear to us the difference between the type of work, or the type of responsibility, or the type of authority, that would have to be exercised, on the one hand by a woman doctor, or a woman teacher, and, on the other hand, by a woman administrative officer?

"(A) An administrative officer has to travel through the bush, and so on, and collect taxes, and he may at any moment be in the midst of a drunken brawl of natives, and so on, and I do not think myself you could ask a woman (personally, if I were Governor of a Colony, I would not ask a woman) to do that, and I would not allow her to do it.

WOMEN SERVANTS OF THE STATE

"(Q) Does it rather come to this, that, whereas a woman educator or a woman medical officer is a person who comes to do an obvious service (she is doing a service to the children; she is obviously a friend of the children; or, if she is a doctor, she is a person who is coming to relieve suffering or illness), if she is an administrative officer she may have to carry out very disagreeable duties, such as that of collecting taxes, and has to have authority to grapple with possibly the most difficult people in the community?

"(A) Yes; I am not saying that there are not women who could not do a great number of these things, but there are certain things in all walks of life which I do not think one would be justified in ordering women to do.

"(Q) You are also taking into account the fact that the position of the native women in the tropical Colonies is very backward?

"(A) In some of them it is very backward indeed.

"(Q) Therefore, at this stage, it might be difficult for a woman to command quite the authority in regard to the collection of taxes, and things of that kind, that she might command fifty years hence, when one hopes that the position of women in these native races will be very much better than it is now?

"(A) I think that is so.

"(Q) At the same time, to have women in these countries as teachers, nurses, and doctors, is bound to help to raise the position of women in these native communities, and perhaps to prepare the way for the day when a woman might be able to carry out the more difficult task of administration?

"(A) Yes, I think that is so. I think women are doing wonderful work in all these colonies."

FUTURE OPPORTUNITIES OF SERVICE

But it was not only Sir Samuel Wilson who felt that women were doing wonderful work in all the Colonies. Other witnesses pointed out that women had for years worked in countries remote from civilization as doctors, teachers, and nurses, and that they had entered uncivilized areas and established friendly relations there; women had also worked as scientists in countries where conditions might be regarded as unsuitable—a woman archaeologist, for example, had supervised gangs of Arab labourers in the Libyan desert; while others had acquired a specialized knowledge of conditions in protectorates and mandated territories.

After due consideration the Tomlin Commission came to the conclusion that women should be eligible for employment in the Dominions Office. Three years later the Committee on Women's Questions recommended that, in the reviews which they suggested should be made in each department, full weight should be given to the views expressed by the Commission in this respect.

Meanwhile women continue to go overseas and render those services permissible to them. To give some recent instances, they have gone to Southern Nigeria, to Lagos, Norfolk Island, North Queensland, and Rhodesia. In Labrador there are many Englishwomen nursing in the back of beyond among the Eskimos and in Australia there are Bush nurses working hundreds of miles away from any city, while in Moyabamba, in Peru, in West Samoa, in British West Africa and Kumasi, there are women teachers.

Exploration continues to attract them and *The Times* of April 2nd, 1938, reported that the well-known traveller Miss Freya Stark had, with a Bedouin escort, travelled in the Hadhramaut, across unknown territory until she reached the town of Azzan. The latter part of this journey was through country inhabited by some of the wildest tribes in the Aden Protectorate. From Azzan, where it is reported she received a warm welcome, she went to the port of Balihaf. "The journey was one of great physical endurance."

But the recommendation of the Tomlin Commission still remains to be carried out. On November 17th, 1936, Mr. Malcolm MacDonald, the Secretary for Dominions Affairs, in reply to a question by Miss Cazalet as to whether he proposed to reserve all appointments in the administrative classes to men only, stated that these "appointments on the administrative establishment of the Dominions Office, which is a joint one with that of the Colonial Office, are reserved to men only." The requirements of the two services, although very different, continue to be regarded as one, and so women, for the time being, are prevented from serving in an administrative capacity either the Colonies or the Dominions. Mr. MacDonald however explained that "the Society for the Oversea Settlement of British Women has since the war been recognized as to all intents and purposes the women's branch of the Oversea Settlement Department of the Dominions Office." Hence his department encourages women to serve overseas, at any rate for some purposes.

In view of the services to the State rendered by women in this country as indicated in this book, it has been asked whether there are no administrative spheres in the Colonies and the Dominions in which public opinion would not welcome the services of women. If, as Sir Samuel Wilson said, "it is now a truism that the duty of trusteeship is the

FUTURE OPPORTUNITIES OF SERVICE

guiding principle of colonial administration," can it be maintained that women have no place in that trusteeship? Are there no problems affecting the welfare of women and children in which the woman administrator should be associated?

The history of women in the Civil Service makes for optimism. Seventy years ago the bold experiment was made of introducing "a few young ladies" into the Post Office; to-day there are about 80,000 women employed throughout the Departments of State and recruited on the same basis as men. It is now widely recognized, that in addition to the contribution which women can make to those questions which particularly affect women and children, their special qualities and gifts can be used and indeed are needed on all sides of the work. It is possible therefore to feel assured that before long there will be still further opportunities for service by the admission of women to the Diplomatic and Consular Services and to the higher grade posts in the Colonial and Dominions Offices. Then indeed and not till then will women be allowed to use their own particular qualifications in the full Service of the State.

IMPORTANT DATES

1870 Entry of women into the Civil Service; employed as telegraph operators.

1871 Women employed as clerks in the Telegraph Clearing House.

1873 Women employed in the Returned Letter Office.

1873 A woman appointed inspector under the Local Government Board.

1875 Women employed in the Savings Bank.

1881 Women clerkships thrown open to public competition.

1883 Directress of Needlework appointed under the Board of Education.

1885 Inspector of Boarded-out Children appointed under the Local Government Board.

1888 Women typists appointed.

1890 Inspector of Domestic Subjects appointed under the Board of Education.

1891 Four women Assistant Commissioners appointed under the Royal Commission on Labour.

1893 Woman Labour Correspondent appointed under the Board of Trade.

1893 Women appointed H.M. Inspectors of Factories under the Home Office.

1896 Women appointed as Sub-Inspectors of Elementary Schools.

1896 Women Inspectors Branch of the Factory Department established.

1897 Woman appointed Assistant Poor Law Inspector.

1899 Women clerks employed in the Board of Education.

WOMEN SERVANTS OF THE STATE

1904 Women clerks employed in the London Telephone Service.

1904 Woman Inspector for Reformatory and Industrial Schools appointed under the Home Office.

1905 Chief Woman Inspector appointed at the Board of Education.

1908 Woman Medical Inspector appointed for Prisons.

1909 Women Trade Board Inspectors appointed under the Board of Trade.

1912 Four Women National Health Insurance Commissioners appointed.

1912 Women National Health Insurance Inspectors appointed.

1913 Woman appointed as Commissioner on the Board of Control.

1915 Report of the Royal Commission on the Civil Service (MacDonnell Commission).

1916 Woman appointed as Chief Inspector of Women's Employment in the Ministry of Labour.

1919 Sex Disqualification (Removal) Act.

1920 Report of the Reorganization Committee (National Whitley Committee).

1921 Aggregation introduced into the Factory Department of the Home Office.

1921 Regulations made under Order in Council regarding employment of married women.

1922 Special competition for the appointment of women to the administrative, executive, and clerical classes.

1924 Women appointed as tax inspectors in the Board of Inland Revenue.

1925 Women appointed (after open competitive examination) to the administrative class.

1927 Aggregation introduced into the Inspectorate Staff of the National Health Insurance Commission.

IMPORTANT DATES

1927 Girls appointed (after open competitive examination) to the clerical classes.

1928 Girls appointed (after open competitive examination) to the executive class.

1931 Report of the Royal Commission on the Civil Service (Tomlin Commission).

1934 Report of the Committee on Women's Questions.

1936 Report of the Committee on the Admission of Women to the Diplomatic and Consular Services.

1937 Report of the Sub-Committee on Sex Differentiation in Pay.

BIBLIOGRAPHY

OFFICIAL PUBLICATIONS

Report on the Re-organization of the Telegraph System in the United Kingdom, 1871.

Report on Post Office Telegraphs, 1872.

Reports and Evidence—Royal Commissions on the Civil Service, 1874-5 (Playfair Commission), 1886-90 (Ridley Commission), 1912-15 (MacDonnell Commission), 1929-31 (Tomlin Commission).

Evidence before the Select Committee on Post Office Servants, 1906 (Hobhouse Committee).

Reports of the Postmaster-General, 1873 and 1874.

Reports of the Local Government Board, 1873-4, 1886, 1899, 1910.

Annual Report of the Chief Inspector of Factories, 1879.

Report of the Departmental Committee on Prisons, 1894.

Report on Children under Five Years of Age in Elementary Schools, 1905.

Report of the Departmental Committee on Reformatory and Industrial Schools, 1913.

Report of the Departmental Committee on the Factory Inspectorate, 1930.

Report on the Administration of the National Health Insurance Act, Part 1.

Report of the Machinery of Government Committee, 1918 (Haldane Committee).

Report of the Committee on Recruitment for the Civil Service after the War, 1919 (Gladstone Committee).

Report of the War Cabinet Committee, 1919.

WOMEN SERVANTS OF THE STATE

Report of the Committee to Enquire into the Organization and Staffing of Government Offices, 1919.

Report of the Committee on the Pay, etc., of State Servants, 1923 (Anderson Committee).

Report of the Reorganization Committee, 1920 (National Whitley Committee).

Introductory Memoranda relating to the Civil Service, submitted by the Treasury, 1930.

Report of the Committee on Women's Questions, 1934.

Report of the Sub-Committee of the National Whitley Committee on Sex Differentiation in Pay, 1937.

Report of the Unemployment Assistance Board, 1935.

Documents relating to the Admission of Women to the Diplomatic and Consular Services, 1934–6.

Hansard, Parliamentary Debates.

GENERAL

The Post Office, by Sir Evelyn Murray, K.C.B. The Whitehall Series. 1927.

The Board of Trade, by Sir Hubert Llewellyn Smith, G.C.B. The Whitehall Series. 1928.

The Home Office, by Sir Edward Troup, K.C.B., K.C.V.O. The Whitehall Series. 1925.

The Ministry of Agriculture and Fisheries, by Sir Francis Floud, K.C.B. The Whitehall Series. 1927.

Women Workers in Seven Professions, edited by Edith J. Morley. 1914.

Women of the War, by Barbara McLaren. 1917.

Women in the Factory, by Dame Adelaide Anderson, D.B.E. 1922.

The Origin and Development of the Inspectorate of the Board of Education, by H. E. Boothroyd. 1923.

BIBLIOGRAPHY

The Romance of Child Reclamation, by M. A. Spielman. 1920.

James Stansfield, A Victorian Champion of Sex Equality, by J. L. and Barbara Hammond. 1932.

A History of the Teaching of Domestic Subjects, by Helen Sillito. 1933.

Women and the Civil Service, by Dorothy Evans. 1934.

"Women as Civil Servants," in *Nineteenth Century*, September 1881.

"Employment of Women in the Public Service," in *Quarterly Review*, January 1881.

"The Young Women at the London Telegraph Office," by Anthony Trollope, in *Good Words*, 1877.

"Civil Service Appointments for Women", by Mr. Cooke Taylor, a paper read at the meeting of the Social Science Congress, Manchester, 1879.

St. Martin's le Grand. April 1913.

Women's Suffrage Journal. September 1872.

"Women in the Courts," in *The Justice of the Peace*, February 1926.

INDEX

Abraham, Miss M. (Mrs. H. J. Tennant), 46, 53, 57, 183
Acland, Rt. Hon. A. H. Dyke, 70
Administrative Grade—employment of women in, 73, 74, 83, 84, 89, 90, 91, 92, 93, 96, 103, 104, 105, 106, 107, 110
Admiralty—employment of women in, 78, 145
Aggregation, 91, 98, 99, 101, 102, 112, 116, 118, 126, 127, 128, 129, 132, 140
Agriculture—
  Fisheries Department, 138
  Ministry of, 66, 78, 79, 137, 138, 139
  Women's Land Army, 79, 137
Air Ministry, employment of women in, 78, 144
Anderson, Dame Adelaide, 47, 55, 57, 58, 182–186, 188
  her publication, *Woman in the Factory—an Administrative Adventure*, 58
Anderson, Sir A. Garrett, Committee on State Servants, etc., 169
Anderson, Sir John, 135
Appeal Tribunals, 129
Arundel Colliver, Mrs., 24
Asquith, Mr. H. H. (Lord Oxford), 53, 55, 61, 82, 94, 130, 183
Astor, Viscountess, 139, 140
Auxiliary Women's Services, 77, 93
Aviation, Civil, 144, 188

Balfour, Mr. Arthur, 32, 180
Bell, Miss Gertrude, 189
Bellhouse, Sir Gerald, 133

Blind Institutions, Inspection of, 118
British Association, report of, 76

Cave, Lord, 58
Cazelet, Miss T., 202
Chalmers, Sir Robert, on employment of women, 69
Chetwynd, Mr., 19, 23, 24
China, Labour conditions in, 184
Civil Servant, definition of, 15
Civil Service Commission, 76, 143, 192
Civilian: The: Post Office Journal, 25
Clerical Assistant Grade (*see* Writing Assistant Class)
Clerical Grades, 85, 89, 90, 91, 94, 96, 109, 110, 111, 114
Colleges for Women (University and Training), 37
Collet, Miss C., 46, 47, 48, 50
Colonial Offices, 197–203
Comptroller and Auditor-General's Department, 45
Comyns, Mr. Patrick, 22, 23, 24
Consular Service, 187, 196, 203
Control, Board of, 78, 119, 143
Cooke-Taylor, Mr., 27, 101
Customs and Excise Department, 79, 143
  Administration of Old Age Pensions Acts, 80, 143

Dale, Mr. F. H. B., 40
Defence Departments, 107, 109
Delevingne, Sir Malcolm, 129, 131
Dickson, Miss I. A., 41, 42, 78
Diplomatic Service, 187–196, 203

WOMEN SERVANTS OF THE STATE

Dominions Office, 197, 201, 203
Durham, Miss F. H., 104

Education, Board of—
 Domestic subjects, inspection of, 36, 37, 38, 41, 42, 43, 121, 122
 Elementary schools, inspection of, 38, 39, 121, 122
 Employment of women inspectors, 36, 38, 39 40, 41, 42, 43, 44, 72, 78, 125
 Employment of women clerks, 29, 44, 45, 72, 109
 Employment of women in administrative grade, 104
 Medical Department, 117, 125
 Organization of the woman inspectorate, 42, 43, 44, 45, 120, 121, 122, 123, 124
 Secondary Schools, inspection of, 41, 43, 121, 122
 Training Colleges, inspection of, 41, 42, 43, 121, 122
Electric and International Telegraph Company, 16
Elliott, Mr. Walter, 139
Emancipation Bill, 87
Englishwoman's Review: quoted, 16
Establishment Lists, 91, 97, 99, 116, 120, 132, 136, 140
 Treasury Committee on, 97
Establishment Officers, 112
Exchequer and Audit Department, 108
Executive Class, 90, 91, 94, 96, 107, 108, 109, 110

"Fair field and no favour," 101
Fawcett, Mr. Henry, 28, 178
Feeble-minded, Royal Commission on, 119
Fisher, Sir Warren, 140, 191
Food, Ministry of, 80
Foreign Office, 66, 78, 192

Girl messengers, 81
Gladstone Committee (Recruitment for the Civil Service after the War), 82, 83, 86, 106, 109, 167
Gladstone, Lord, 62, 137
Good Words, article on "The Young Women at the London Telegraph Office," 27
Government Actuary's Department, 109

Haldane Committee (Machinery of Government), 82, 83, 167
Haldane, Viscount, 70, 82
Hammond, Mr. and Mrs. J. L., 30
Hankin, Mr. S. T., 124
Headmistresses, Association of, 77
Health Insurance Commission, 63, 64, 117
 Employment of women, 29, 48, 64, 72, 109
 Organization of the woman inspectorate, 64, 118, 119
 Report on Administration of Act, 65
 Women Insurance Commissioners, 64, 72
Health for Scotland, Department of, 105
Health of Women, 24, 84
Health, Ministry of, 105, 117, 120
 District Audit Staff, 109, 120
 Medical Department, 125
Henderson, Sir Vivian, 133, 135
Hills, Major, 92, 94, 96, 139, 150, 151, 168
Hoare, Sir Samuel, 88, 94, 151
Hobhouse, Mr. C. H., 163
Hobhouse Committee (Select Committee on Post Office Servants), 29

INDEX

Holt Committee (Select Committee on Post Office Servants), 29
Home Office—Factory Department, 48, 129
   Chief Inspector of, 1879, 51, 52, 56, 129, 136
   Children's Branch, 136
   Medical Branch, 136
   Probation Branch, 137
   Reformatory and Industrial Schools, 58, 59, 60
   Women Inspectors of Factories, 51, 53, 54, 55, 56, 57, 58, 73, 76, 78, 129, 130, 131, 132, 133, 134, 135, 136, 141, 183
Honours for Women, 179

India Office, employment of women in, 78
Industrial Museums, Conference of directors, 136
Inland Revenue, Board of, 65, 66, 140, 141, 142
   Estate Duty Office, 108, 140, 142, 143
International Labour Organization, 126, 136, 184, 189

Justice of the Peace: Women and the Courts, 56

Labour, Ministry of, 48, 104, 109, 125, 126, 127, 128
Labour, Royal Commission on, 183
   Appointment of four women Assistant Commissioners, 46, 53
Land Registry, 143, 145
Lawrence, Hon. Maude, 40, 41, 42, 112
Lawyers, Women, 143

Leathes, Sir Stanley, 70
Llewellyn Smith, Sir Herbert, 48
Local Government Board, 29, 30, 32, 117
   Reports of, 31, 32, 34, 36
Lunacy Commission, 119

MacDonald, Malcolm M., 202
MacDonnell (Royal Commission on the Civil Service), 45, 48, 58, 68, 69, 70, 71, 72, 73, 74, 77, 149, 166, 168
McKenna, Mr. R., 55
McLaren, Sir Charles, 69
Machinery of Government Committee, 82, 83, 167
Married women, employment of, 21, 48, 99, 146, 147, 148, 149, 150, 151, 152, 153, 154, 155, 156, 157
Mason, Miss M. H., 32, 33, 34, 35, 36, 180–182, 188
Medical Women, 142
Mill, John Stuart, 187
Montgomery, Sir Hubert, 190, 191
Morant, Sir Robert, 39, 40, 41, 42, 44, 63, 120, 122
Mundella, Mr. H. J., 46, 47
Munitions, Ministry of, 80, 81
Murray, Sir Evelyn, 115
Museums, employment of women in, 144

National Education Board for Ireland, employment of women inspectors, 44
National Farmers' Union, 139
National Savings Committee, 143
National Service Department, 78
Newman, Sir George, 117
Nineteenth Century, article on "Women as Civil Servants," 27, 159

215

WOMEN SERVANTS OF THE STATE

Old Age Pension Officers, 143
Organization and Staffing of Government Offices Committee, 85
Overseas Settlement for British Women, Society for, 202

Paterson, Mrs. Emma Ann, 51
Paterson, Miss Mary M., 53
Pensions, Ministry of, 80, 104
Phipps, Sir Edmund, 45
Playfair (Royal Commission on the Civil Service), 21, 25, 147
Poor Law Administration—
   Boarding-out system, 30, 32, 33, 34, 35, 36, 117, 181
   Inspectors, 30, 32, 33, 34, 35, 36, 73
   Institutions, 30, 31, 32, 35
Postmaster-General, Reports of, 20, 21, 25
Post Office—
   Accountant-General's Department, 114
   Money Order Department, 28, 114
   Postal Censorship, 79
   Postal Order Branch, 28
   Postal Service, 115, 159
   Returned Letter Office, 21, 24
   Savings Bank, 24, 25, 28, 29, 114, 177, 178, 179
   Telegraph Clearing House Branch, 19, 24
   Telegraph Service, 15, 16, 17, 18, 30, 115, 116, 158, 161, 162, 163
   Telephone Service, 28, 115
Post Office, employment of women in, 71, 73, 80, 109, 110, 114, 115
Post Office Servants, Select Committee of (Hobhouse), 163

Post Office Women Clerks, Association of, 162, 163
Prisons—
   Commission, 61, 62, 137
   Inspection of, 59, 60, 61, 62, 63, 73
Public Record Office, 105
Public Trustee, employment of women in, 29, 72, 143, 145

Quarterly Review: article on "Employment of Women in the Public Service," 27, 160

Recruitment of Women, 28, 68, 81, 82, 83, 84, 85, 86, 90, 92, 104
Registrar-General's Office, employment of women, 29, 72
Regulations governing appointment of women, 95, 96
Remuneration of women, 24, 64, 68, 73, 85, 158, 159, 160, 161, 162, 163, 164, 165, 166, 167, 168, 169, 170, 171, 172, 173
Reorganization Committee, 89, 90, 91, 93, 96, 97, 98, 99, 103, 107, 108, 109, 110, 111, 126, 168
Reservation of Posts, 99, 100, 101, 102
Ridley (Royal Commission on the Civil Service), 29, 65, 66
Ridley, Sir M. White, 55
Ritson, Miss M., 105
Robinson, Sir Arthur, 118
Robinson, Sir Malcolm, 131

Schuster, Sir Claud, 192
Scientific Research, Department of, 144
Scottish Education Department, employment of women inspectors, 44

INDEX

Scudamore, Mr., 17, 19, 20, 102, 136, 146, 157, 158, 161, 162, 173
Segregation, 91, 98, 99, 110, 112, 116, 118, 126, 128, 140
Selby-Bigge, Sir L. A., views on employment of women, 45, 70
Senior, Mrs. Nassau, 30, 31, 32
Sex Differention in Pay Committee, 172, 173
Sex Disqualification (Removal) Act, 87, 88, 91, 92, 93, 99, 150, 151, 187, 191
Orders in Council, 93, 100, 152, 153, 187
Shaftesbury, Lord, 16, 51
Shorthand and Typing Grades (*see* Typing Grade), 65, 90, 91, 110, 111
Smith, Mr. G. R., 21, 147
Smith, Miss M. C., 26, 27, 29, 34, 44, 45, 176-180, 183
Social Science Congress in Manchester, 27, 101
Special Post for Women, 112, 113
Squire, Miss Rose, 55
Stansfield, Miss I., 34, 35, 36, 117
Stansfield, Mr. James, 30, 31, 32
Stark, Freya, Miss, 202
State Servants, Pay and other Conditions, Committee on, 169
Stationery Office, 78
Superannuation, 149, 173, 174, 175
Sweated Industries Exhibition, 1906...49
Sweating System, chief features of, 46, 50
Symonds, Sir Aubrey, 122

Taylor, Mr. Theodore, 55
Tennant, Mrs. H. J. (*see* Abraham, Miss M.)

Thomas, Sir Charles Howell, 138
Tomlin Commission (Royal Commission on the Civil Service), 100, 101, 111, 115, 116, 119, 121, 124, 127, 135, 138, 139, 140, 141, 143, 153, 154, 155, 157, 170, 173, 174, 189, 191, 197, 201, 202
Trade, Board of—
Administrative grade, 105
Collection of labour statistics, 46, 47
Conciliation Department, 50, 79
Labour Department, 47, 48, 49, 72, 79, 125
Labour Exchanges, 48, 49, 50, 72, 79
Trade Boards Act, 50
Trade Boards Inspectors appointed, 50, 126, 127
Trades Union Congress General Council, 134
Training of Women, Society for Promoting, 16
Transport, Ministry of, 145
Treasury, Women on Staff, 74, 85, 104
Trollope, Anthony, 27
Troup, Sir Edward, 58
Truck System, 49
Typing Grades, 65, 72, 110, 111, 147, 148

Unemployment Assistance Board, 128
University Women—
Employment of, 77, 78, 107
Federation of, 76

Victoria, Queen, 15, 16

Wamsley, Miss L. W., 117, 118
War Cabinet Committee, 85, 168

War Office, employment of women in, 76, 78
War Period—
  Number of women employed, 75, 76, 81
  Reasons for increase, 75
War Savings Department, 80
Ward, Mr. Leonard, 135
Ward, Sir E. W. D., views on employment of women, 71
Welsh Board of Health, 117
Whitley Councils, 89, 102, 113, 116, 120, 126, 139, 172, 174
Wilson, Sir Samuel, 197, 201, 203
Women, employment of, 17, 18, 19, 20, 21, 22, 23, 24, 25, 26, 29, 34, 42
Women of the War, by Barbara McLaren, 82
Women's Questions, Committee on, 102, 128, 139, 155, 156, 201
Women Workers in Seven Professions, 145
Workhouse Nursing Association, 34
Writing Assistant Class, 90, 110

...duct Safety Concerns and Information please contact our EU ...entative GPSR@taylorandfrancis.com
...or & Francis Verlag GmbH, Kaufingerstraße 24, 80331 München, Germany

www.ingramcontent.com/pod-product-compliance
Lightning Source LLC
Chambersburg PA
CBHW050633300426
44112CB00012B/1782

For Product Safety Concerns and Information please contact our EU
representative GPSR@taylorandfrancis.com
Taylor & Francis Verlag GmbH, Kaufingerstraße 24, 80331 München, Germany

www.ingramcontent.com/pod-product-compliance
Lightning Source LLC
Chambersburg PA
CBHW050633300426
44112CB00012B/1782